TROUT FRIENDS

TROUT FRIENDS

Bill Stokes

Illustrations by Owen Coyle

PRAIRIE OAK PRESS
Madison, Wisconsin

First edition, first printing

Prairie Oak Press
821 Prospect Place
Madison, Wisconsin 53703
Email: popjama@aol.com

Typeset by Quick Quality Press, Madison, Wisconsin
Cover photographs by Brent Nicastro
Printed in the United States of America
by Sheridan Books, Chelsea, Michigan

Library of Congress Cataloging-In-Publication Data

Stokes, Bill, 1931–
Trout friends/Bill Stokes ; illustrations by Owen Coyle.--1st ed.
p. cm.
ISBN 1-879483-66-1
1. Trout fishing--Wisconsin--Anecdotes. I. Title.
SH688.U6 S74 2000
799.1'757--dc21 00–026328

CONTENTS

PREFACE

Since trout fishing—or any kind of fishing—is not innate, we must be taken by the hand and led to the still and raging waters. Over the course of a lifetime, those who lead us become the big ones that get away, and brooding over their mortality and your own is a constant temptation.

But it would be a dumb thing to do. Better to get out on a stream somewhere and feel the presence of the old wormers and others in the backcast that inexplicably snags on every last alder twig.

Then in the exquisite environs of trout, you can hear their voices and be with them again.

What I know as trout fishing was shaped by an incredible lineup of uncles, neighborhood geezers, and extraordinary friends. The collective lesson I learned from them—belatedly, of course—was that all things are cyclic, and the cycles are unbelievably brief. Therefore, you are obliged to have as much fun, frivolity, and fishing as possible before you end up like a spent mayfly, drifting with the current until the big trout takes you down.

For Betty,

who called it "trout floundering"

THE GOOD LIE

YOU NEVER KNOW who plants the earliest seeds of trout fishing, but certainly the first person who takes you to a river plants some. Ben Lusby did that for me, and sometimes now when the musty smells of winter are being sorted out by the first warm breezes, I swear that I get a whiff of Mr. Lusby's pipe smoke. It is strong, like the breath of an old bear that never quite makes it out of hibernation, and its mysterious presence renders me pretty much useless for a day or so. To to get back on track I have to go through the redhorse spring again, rejoicing in the memory of it and wondering how a lie can not only stand up to the rigors of the decades but somehow become a thing of beauty.

That spring came up the Yellow River in a lime green prom dress, tossing plum blossom corsages at the high banks while an avian chorus made romantic claims in the bottom land. It was celebratory, as usual, and the blanket invitation to participate pulled earthworms out from under the decaying leaves and made the red-tailed hawk scream with procreative energy.

Just up from the river, at the little brown house on the end of the block, Mr. Lusby's cats lolled on the doorstep and feigned disinterest in the raging libido of the season. They were not fooling anyone and certainly not me because I had heard them howling and moaning and fighting in the night until I was sure that their catamount ancestors had invaded the neighborhood and were about to come leaping out of the darkness to crash through the window into my bedroom. I hated those cats, but by day they were only arrogant creatures who ignored me with a grandeur I could never duplicate, and who occasionally awoke from their naps to stare at Mr. Lusby's son Alvin because he was the one most likely to see that they got something to eat.

Alvin was twenty or thirty years old—it was hard to tell exactly, and he had never gone to school. People said he was "not right," and since I was too young to know what that meant I tended to ignore the community assessment and agree with the infernal cats that Alvin was fine, even though the right side of his body was twisted and his face was crooked, and sometimes when it seemed that he should say something he just smiled his lopsided smile and then looked down at his feet.

For several days that spring Alvin and Mr. Lusby had walked past our house in the late afternoon, Mr. Lusby looking like a summer version of Santa Claus with a huge bulging burlap bag slung over his shoulder and Alvin limping along behind with a couple of fish poles.

Caught in the purgatory of a preschooler, I had watched them from our front porch, speculating that the burlap bag was full of fish, never having nerve enough to ask. And then one day when I was out by the sidewalk with my coaster wagon, Mr. Lusby stopped and said, "That wagon would be just right for hauling fish."

Before I could react, he flopped the damp burlap sack down into the wagon so that its top flared open and fish spilled out as if they had some place to go. They were football-sized fish with scales as big as dimes and pucker mouths that looked as if they spent their time kissing the bottom. Their sudden appearance had startled me and I stepped back and stared down at them as Mr. Lusby removed the pipe from his mouth and laughed.

"Come on, Billy," Mr. Lusby said. "Haul our fish home."

And so just like that I became one of them, magically metamorphosed from the boring ranks of spectator to participant with the simple flop of a fish sack. It was akin to being plucked off a tricycle to ride with Hopalong Cassidy.

I pulled the wagon down the street and into the cluttered yard behind the little brown house, feeling as if life had suddenly taken on some of the meaning that had heretofore only fluttered around the periphery like confused bats. And then I watched in open-mouthed fascination as Mr. Lusby cleaned the fish, using his knife to flick the guts over toward the cats while Alvin with his one good arm hung the cleaned carcasses in the dilapidated little smoke shanty.

"Redhorse," Mr. Lusby said. "Bony, but good when they're smoked."

One of the cats growled like a dog, and Alvin laughed his funny, jerky laugh as the cat lashed out with a quick paw and sent one of the other cats into squalling retreat beneath the house.

Mr. Lusby glanced up and said, "You oughta come with us, Billy."

That was all it took, of course, and the next morning—after a sleepless night that was due more to simmering excitement than to caterwauling cats—I was waiting out in front of the house, suffering the indignity of an accompanying mother who wanted a few more details from Mr. Lusby.

"We want him for his wagon," Mr. Lusby said, grinning down at me, "and we think we can make a fisherman of him."

He satisfied my mother that he would not let me fall into the river and then we headed off down the street, Mr. Lusby leading the way, me next with the wagon, and Alvin bringing up the rear with the fish poles. At the end of the street, we crossed the highway and headed down the dirt trail that led to the river, and as the canopy of brush and trees closed overhead I knew the sensation of shunning childhood as if it were a wet diaper. I looked back in time to see Alvin stumble and then catch himself as he grinned at me.

Then the soft gurgle of the river's current wrapped around us like tentacles and we walked downstream to a grassy bank where a male blackbird fluttered overhead in a frenzy of indignation.

"This is the place," Mr. Lusby said, and he and Alvin separated the fish poles, baited the hooks with gobs of squirming night crawlers, swung the baits out into the current, and then propped the poles with rocks so that they stuck out over the river.

"That pole is yours," Mr. Lusby said, gesturing at the shortest pole. "Watch the end and when it starts jerking, grab the pole and pull."

I sat next to the pole with the coiled energy of a hunting cat, and then it seemed to me that almost immediately the tip began to wiggle and so I grabbed on and hauled the fish pole up with such energy that the bait sailed up and tangled in the branches of a willow tree.

There was no fish. There had been no fish, and I knew that the minute the hook and sinker had wound themselves tightly around the overhead branches. I had been too anxious and I tried to smile back at Mr. Lusby and Alvin as they laughed.

"The big one got away," Mr. Lusby said, and laughed again.

Alvin shinnied up the slanting trunk of the willow—almost falling once but pulling with his good arm to regain his balance. He jerked my line loose and then we were all three fishing again. Twice more I was sure that a fish had swallowed my bait and each time my energetic reaction tangled the fish line in the willow. And each time Alvin would patiently retrieve it and grin at me.

Mr. Lusby caught the first fish and he whooped and hollered as he made his fish pole almost bend double, and then grabbed the line to slide a glistening redhorse up onto the grass. The fish flopped and worked its gills in and out, and its pucker mouth opened and closed as if it were looking for a kiss. I had never before seen anyone catch a fish and it was hard to believe that the gurgling river held such mysterious creatures.

"They're still runnin'," Mr. Lusby said as he put the redhorse into the gunny bag and rebaited his hook. And then again my hook was tangled up in the willow branches. But Alvin was onto a fish before he could help me out, and he fought it with his fish pole hooked under his bad arm and the other arm pulling as hard as he could, his lopsided grin bigger than usual and his good leg braced out in front of him. Before Alvin had even landed his fish Mr. Lusby caught another one, and then it was Alvin's turn again, and it went on like that—fast and furious, so they didn't even have time to put the fish into the bag and there were fish flopping all over the bank.

I stood in the middle of it in a state of mild shock, so amazed by the strange activity all around me that I forgot about my fish line tangled in the tree.

And then it was over. The fish quit biting as if a switch had been flipped. Mr. Lusby picked up the fish and put them in the burlap bag which he tied to an alder down by the water, and then he looked at me and at my line in the tree and said, "Billy, we gotta get you fishin' before they start biting again."

But they didn't start. We sat there for hours, through a lunch of baloney sandwiches and through Mr. Lusby's nap, during which he snored so loud he sounded like a truck. When he woke up he looked around and said, "They better start biting pretty soon."

But they didn't and the hours of inactivity had evaporated my enthusiasm for fishing until I meandered off looking for frogs. I glanced back to see Mr. Lusby watching me carefully, and once I saw him lift my pole and look at the bait.

Suddenly I heard him shout, "Billy! Billy! Come on. You got a fish."

I turned and ran toward him and as I did so I knew suddenly what he had done. I don't know how I knew it—not from a clear sensory assessment because I hadn't seen or heard enough for that but from something in that spring day and in the fishing bond among the three of us. I knew with a certainty beyond all doubt that Mr. Lusby had taken one of the redhorse out of the fish sack and hooked it onto my line and released it and then he had hollered, "Billy! Billy!"

But then I was fighting the fish—hauling back on the fish pole with all of my strength while Mr. Lusby watched and shouted advice. "Hang on to him, Billy. Don't give him any slack."

If the fish fought with any less vigor because it was the unfortunate creature's second bout of the day, I did not notice, and then the redhorse was on the bank and I stared down at it and Mr. Lusby patted me on the back and exclaimed that maybe my fish was the biggest of the day.

I knew as I stood there looking down at the fish that I had bought into a lie, but I also knew that there was nothing that I wanted to do about it. I had, after all, caught the fish, and the technical aspects of just what is involved in "catching" were beyond me so there wasn't anything I could have done about it even if I had wanted to.

None of this, of course, was ever manifested in any kind of an inner struggle. I was much too young for such things, and I loved the lie even more than Mr. Lusby who had created it.

And then I loved it even more when we walked down the sidewalk in front of the houses on our block and Mr. Lusby told an inquiring neighbor that I had caught the biggest fish. He told my parents the same thing, and I didn't want to look at him in case he winked at my father.

Later, in Mr. Lusby's backyard, I watched again as the fish were cleaned, and Mr. Lusby said it was my job to hand the fish to Alvin so he could hang them in the smoker. It was hard to hang onto the slippery fish, and when I dropped one of them in front of him, Alvin bent down and his crooked grin was so close I could see the stray whiskers around his lips.

"Good fisherman," he said, and squeezed my shoulder with his good hand.

Sometimes in the spring when I get that strange whiff of Mr. Lusby's pipe smoke I can feel the pressure of Alvin's fingers, and then I know how incredibly lucky I have been to have lived all these years with such a special lie.

FISH TRAUMA

ONE VERY DARK June night as I stood in the middle of the Yellow River on the end of a fast and furious hex hatch, a beaver bumped my leg and then slapped its tail so hard that it was like a hand grenade exploding under my nose. On another moonless night as I waded the edge of a deep Willow Creek pool, a cackling rooster pheasant rocketed up out of the very hummock that I had grasped to steady myself.

These nerve-shattering things are forever happening to fishermen, expecially trout fishermen, and when they do, I think about Uncle Duffy and how he taught me that there are some things about fishing that can startle you so bad you think you are going to die, or maybe wet your pants first and then die.

It began one morning with soft, warm rain drifting over the window of the upstairs bedroom where I slept. That bedroom in my grandparents' old farmhouse was like a womb, the quiet darkness its warm amnion and the faint stirring in the rest of the house an umbilical of reassurance. Within its confines a boy could dismiss life with a yawn and tumble effortlessly into the bottomless chasm of dreams, sinking and falling ever deeper until he was one with nothing and only a dream himself. And from the depths of such serene slumber the trip to wakefulness was an agony, even an impossibility.

"Billy! Billy! Wake up. We're going fishing."

The words were as moths fluttering against glass, weak, absurd things that could never accomplish their purpose.

"Billy! Billy!" And then the words came with a gentle shake that made the bedsprings squeak. "Come on. We gotta get goin' while it's still raining."

Uncle Duffy was talking. He of the round, smiling face and the big hands and the judgment to do the right thing with a rainy day.

So the fishing began, on a day when spitting rain interrupted the sweaty season of making hay, and farmers paused like foxes sniffing the wind. Grandpa Helgeland was one of them, and he stood by the kitchen door gazing out across the fields.

"We could fix the pasture fence," he said, but there was no conviction in his voice. It was not in him to spend time in such frivolity as fishing, but his adult son did not see it that way and Grandpa knew it. Uncle Duffy loved to fish, and if he used the excuse of entertaining a visiting nephew, that might have made the fishing more palatable to Grandpa, who was, if anything, a kind man who wanted happiness for those around him.

The fog of sleep had lifted layer by layer as I tugged on clothes and stumbled down the varnished stairs to the breakfast table. I sat and watched rich, creamy milk cut tiny white rivers through the brown sugar and oatmeal while a doting grandmother issued a stream of cautions about the fishing trip.

"You be careful and don't stand up in the boat," she said, giving me a stern look, a smile, and a sugar doughnut all at the same time.

The bamboo fish poles were tied to the passenger side of the car, and I could see them slanting up over the rear window of the dusty old Ford, their tips permanently bent from what I imagined to be prolonged battles with huge fish.

The day wrapped everything in gray mist, warm and delicate, and as we drove along it swirled up behind the car like lines of shy dancers jerked suddenly to their feet. I was awake then, more so than I might ever have been. The combination of new circumstance and experience and the pain of exquisite anticipation was almost unbearable.

The car hummed down the road as if it had eyes and did not need the guidance of Uncle Duffy hunched over the steering wheel. I looked out the window at the fence posts zipping past in an endless retreat and at the fields that glistened with the rain. And it was as if the watery world of toothy, hard-eyed fish was somehow coming to meet us, the lakes and rivers having fragmented and shattered to move over the land and accommodate life forms that did not have fins or gills. I shivered with the prospect of that and remembered once when Uncle Duffy had stopped to show my parents a huge northern pike that he had caught. The fish had seemed to fill the entire car trunk, and I had looked suddenly over the rim of the trunk and directly into a huge round, obsidian eye that had burned its image like a brand onto my spongy young brain. That Uncle Duffy and I were now about to enter into the realm of such fearsome, evil-eyed monsters threatened to wind my metabolic spring far beyond the limits of its resilience.

And then it happened: the frayed binder twine holding the front of the fish poles to one of the Ford's headlights broke and there was a sudden crackling and crunching and a whirl of splintered bamboo fragments hurtling past the car windows.

"Damn," Uncle Duffy muttered and slammed his foot down on the brake pedal.

I wasn't sure what had happened, but as the car slowed and finally stopped, I looked out to see the fish poles hanging in a sad tangle from the door handle. My heart—a moment ago soaring like an osprey over hapless trophy fish—shattered like the brittle bamboo poles. There could be no fishing now. It had ended before it had even started, and I watched as Uncle Duffy ripped the broken poles from the car and flung them into the ditch.

He got back into the driver's seat with a scowl and we started down the road again. Why hadn't we turned around and gone back home? We had no fish poles so certainly we could not go fishing. I slouched down in the seat and glanced over at Uncle Duffy. Incredibly, he was smiling!

"Those poles were too old to handle big fish anyway," he said. "We'll get some new ones."

Reprieve! The day was an emotional roller coaster and all I could do was hang on.

We stopped at the hardware store and the new fish poles that Uncle Duffy bought were strong and straight, without the bends from previous fish fights, and the bald-headed man in the store said they were guaranteed to catch only big fish.

"Big ones like that," he said, and gestured over his shoulder toward a huge stuffed fish that hung on the back wall. It was a northern pike, brown with age and its back thick with dust. It was mounted with its jaws spread wide so that its sawlike teeth showed plainly in an awful leer, and one of its glass eyes glared out at the cluttered store with awesome defiance. And hanging from the fish's front teeth by a frayed shoestring was a child's shoe.

"We don't know what happened to the kid who was wearing that shoe," the storekeeper said, glancing at me, and then over at Uncle Duffy. And then they laughed.

"Don't hang your feet over the side of the boat," the storekeeper said as we left the store, and Uncle Duffy grinned and looked down at me.

"We won't," he said, and I smiled back at him, even though I was not totally sure just where fish jesting and facts went their separate ways.

Then we were on the lake, suspended over the still water like an odd space creature in the fog, the new fish poles protruding over the sides as antennae, and the oars like embryonic wings that Uncle Duffy powered with slow, steady strokes. Spoon baits with feathered treble hooks were attached to the heavy green lines and tossed over the side, and sometimes their flickering shine could be seen down in the water. And each time there was a brief sighting of one of the whirling spoons I knew that certainly a giant fish was about to clamp its gaping, toothy jaws around it and there would then ensue a terrific battle. My head and shoulders ached with the fearful prospect.

The shoreline trees faded in and out of view with the shifting of the fog, and the boat left a trail of lines and circles on the surface of the dark water as Uncle Duffy rowed along just outside of the lily pads.

Then a loon called suddenly from very close by, a wild, cackling yodel that could only express the lunacy of something evil and destructive. I almost jumped out of the boat.

"Just a loon," Uncle Duffy said. "Must have a nest nearby."

And then while my scalp felt as if it were sprouting quills, the fish pole in front of me suddenly bent into a sharp arc that throbbed and bounced as if it were being tortured. I could only watch it, paralyzed with fascination and fear for what might be out there under the black water with enough power to cause so much commotion—something with eyes as hard as blue steel and with teeth like rows of needles.

"Grab the pole! Grab the pole!" Uncle Duffy shouted, and when I simply stared down at the thick end of the fish pole that jumped up and down in front of me, Uncle Duffy made a desperate lunge for it just as the pole thumped over the side and slid into the water. Like a slim spear propelled by an invisible force, the fish pole sliced along the surface and then slowly submerged into the tangle of lily pads.

"Why didn't you grab it?" Uncle Duffy said, watching as the pole disappeared.

I could not answer. There was no answer. I had failed the very basic test of a fisherman: I had declined the opportunity to engage, to go one-on-one with whatever was out there on the end of the line, to fight it on its own terms and to try to bring it to the boat and ultimately to the admiring eyes of family members and finally to the table where the fish and I would be the center of attention.

It all went through my mind—the immensity of the opportunity, the abject, humiliating failure, and the fear that had spawned it. I wanted to melt away, like hot butter, and never have to face myself or anyone else ever again. I could not look at Uncle Duffy and I stared down at my feet and at the place where the fish pole had been propped against the side of the boat.

Uncle Duffy began rowing again, slowly and rhythmically, and the creaking of the oarlocks was the only sound anywhere in the world. He rowed for a long time, and then the mist turned to big raindrops that came down harder so that little streams of water began to run down inside my clothes, which was a good thing for someone whose nether region dampness had preceded the downpour.

FIRST FISHING FRIEND

WE WERE GOING to die! Just above the "dead waters" where Engle Creek gets fat and lazy before joining the Yellow River, we were going to die. The swirling flood of the creek was going to creep up out of its boggy bed and drown us like rats. And if the cold, sucking water didn't get us, we were going to be fried by one of those blinding explosions of lightning.

Our lives would have flashed before our eyes except that we were so young there wasn't much to flash. And so we huddled in vacuous fear beneath the collapsed tent, bug-eyed, whimpering, and waiting for the end. It was Rob's fault. It usually was. He had gotten us into this. But what difference would that make when they found our young sodden bodies twisted among the alder and mud?

"We're goners," Rob said, lifting his head briefly and then ducking as a bolt of lightning streaked overhead.

Rob! Rob! At least we were going together. That was fitting: First fishing friends, and friends to the end.

There's something about that first-fishing-friend—that one of your own generation who is as innocent and naive and as dumb as you are. And though you cannot know it at the time, nor even be aware of it later, the first-fishing-friend becomes the measure that finds all subsequent fishing companions strangely wanting. It was that way with Cousin Rob. There could not have been a better fishing pal, and I stand by that assessment even though in the end, Rob left me holding a can of freshly dug worms and went off down the road to see Delores Hanson.

I was two years younger than Rob, and so it was at least that long before I had any inkling of what was behind his aberrant behavior in choosing a girl over me and those juicy fishing worms. I worried that Rob had somehow come unglued and I wondered if it might have had something to do with our "test pilot" escapade when he rode an old, out-of-control baby buggy down the pasture hill and made a spectacular and unplanned dive into a summer-ripe manure pile.

Later, when biology executed its hammerlock and cut off the air supply to my own brain, I forgave Rob. Not completely, of course, because when fishing friends decide to give up fishing for something else they should do it together.

(Taken on a global level, puberty has obviously saved so many fish that it should probably be a canon of fish management: *Fishing pressure in any given geographic area will be in inverse proportion to the number of boys who attain puberty during the preceding year.*)

But before Rob and I became victims of the grim replicater we had those golden years of fishing, that all too brief time after a boy has gnawed through the apron strings, and adults worry less about where he is and what he is doing and more about what he will bring home and whether it will be dead or alive.

Rob had the advantage of living just up the sand hill from Engle Creek, the Anderson farm perching as it did on the high bank where the last glacial torrent had crested ten thousand years ago, and where, over the millenniums, lumbering old snapping turtles had come to lay their eggs. That proximity to fishing opportunity and his age advantage made Rob the natural leader in most of our fishing escapades. And they began, of course, on Engle Creek, a little clear-water brook trout stream that slithered quietly through the hummocks to the "golumpity-glump" of American bitterns and the whistling wings of acrobatic snipe.

Rob's home and Engle Creek were a hilly, two and one-half mile, dogleg bike ride from our home farm. I could do that ride in about thirty minutes depending on the wind, the condition of the gravel road—muddy or dusty—and the alertness of the neighbors' bike-chasing dogs.

However long the trip took, Rob would be waiting, usually down by the big hole just below the washed-out bridge. There he would be lolling on the grass or wading in the shallows or sitting with his feet in the water while a worm-baited hook soaked in the cold stream. His grin was always wide and his summer haircut was always so short that his head—like the rest of him—turned brown from the sun and in his sinewy configuration he looked like a cheerful weasel. Once I found him hanging by his knees from the rickety footbridge, his head only inches above the water and his arms dangling down into the ripples.

"It's like being a fish," he said. "Try it."

And so the two of us hung there upside down, feeling the thrill of being a brook trout and reveling in the reversed view of the landscape until Rob's older brother Edgar came along and said if we hung there too long our brains would turn to mush, which, he implied, would not be all that much of a transition.

Rob and I shared so many good times that it is difficult to sort them out, but the camping trip that took us down to the Dead Waters and the encounter with the thunderstorm were typical. That venture, teetering as it did on the edge of calamity and producing enough raw fear to ferment adrenaline, is the kind of experience that you can never know as an adult.

Our secret plan—only elements of which we shared with our doubting parents—had been to explore the route of the creek down to where it joined the river, and to fish and camp along the way. We packed food into a canvas grain sack until it weighed too much for either one of us to lift, and so the larder had to be cut down by several large cans of fruit cocktail, five pounds of potatoes, great quantities of other commodities, and the cast-iron frying pan.

We started out on a sun-washed afternoon when cumulus clouds were soaring over summer like a pillow fight, and a concert of bird song swept up and down the creek bottom. The first few hundred yards were easy, fueled as we were by the sheer excitement of the venture. We staggered between the bogs along the stream, stumbling under our outrageous burdens, and then somehow the unmanageable sack with the food and camping gear fell into the soft black slurry of a little feeder stream. We were an hour extracting it and rearranging our gear, and when it was done we were covered with mud and scratches.

Rob said that to make better time we had to climb up the bank and follow the creek from the high ground. It was a gasping, panting struggle up out of the nettles and alder and then up the steep, grass-covered hill where the Anderson cows stood and stared at us with their long, sad bovine faces.

Rob tried to chase the cows away because, as he put it, he just didn't want them watching us.

We followed a cow trail along the side hill, and when Rob slipped on some fresh cow dung, he cursed an adult curse and chased the cows again. I had the feeling that somebody else's cows might not have been so bad, but we were being followed and stared at by the cows that knew Rob personally and that he in turn knew by their given names. This seemed to detract from Rob's ability to fully enjoy our adventure.

We finally crossed the fence out of the pasture into Wicker's Woods, and while we were no longer bothered by cows, there was the impossible tangle of blackberry briars. By evening we had made it only to the Dead Waters, a flat marshy area where Engle Creek lost its hydrologic drive and more or less lolled among the bogs to delay its meeting with the Yellow River.

We pitched the tent at the foot of the hill, next to one of the spring ponds, and only the black mud that covered our exposed skin saved us from losing every last drop of blood to millions of mosquitoes. A smudge fire helped after we finally got it started, but it didn't protect us from inhaling the mosquitoes, and finally we both made a dive for the tent and went into a slapping frenzy to kill the hundreds of mosquitoes that had made the dive with us.

Supper was cold beans—which we could reach without leaving the tent—and the one can of fruit cocktail that had survived the day-long jettisoning of supplies.

And then it got darker than it has ever gotten in the history of darkness and we could not find the candles. Something made a series of tremendous splashes in the pond—Rob said it was probably some of the big trout—and then out of the night there came a hideous, high-pitched scream. In the solid darkness of the tent, the scream seemed to take on a persona so that there was Rob and there was me and then there was the awful scream filling all the rest of the space. Rob and I grabbed at each other and I'm not sure but what we didn't scream too. The scream went on and on, getting more shrill and piercing until suddenly it ended as if a great, shaggy throat had been cut.

"What the . . . ?" Rob whispered, his voice shaking.

The scream was obviously nothing more than a cottontail rabbit dying in the clutches of a predator, probably a great horned owl. But it was nothing so harmless that night. It was a starved panther about to dine on a couple of terrified boys, and as the seconds of relative silence ticked on, Rob and I huddled together and waited for the slashing claws and the fangs. When they didn't come and the other night sounds filtered into the tent, Rob said, "We gotta get outa here."

"It's too dark," I said. "We couldn't find our way."

Before Rob could respond, the darkness was rent by a mighty blast of white light and an incredible explosion of sound. It was as if the fires of hell had lashed out to envelop us. It had been a bolt of lightning, and it signaled the abrupt arrival of a thunderstorm that began to whip through the trees and underbrush with such force that the tent flattened around us like a cape. And then the rain came, in torrents and buckets. Along with it there was such a sustained blast of lightning and cracking thunder that it seemed as if a shattered kind of daylight was trying to make a comeback.

In the midst of it—with the sodden tent plastered around us and the wind and lightning whipping at us—Rob shouted, "The creek's gonna flood and drown us."

As wet as we were and as vulnerable to the whims of the thunderstorm, the prospect of drowning in the middle of the dark night seemed suddenly inevitable and even strangely appealing: at least it would be different from the present misery.

The storm built to an cataclysmic climax of white light and earth-shaking thunder. And then slowly it abated, the thunder fading to a grumbling rumble in the distance as the lightning flashes lost their brilliance. Rob and I huddled together and waited for the water to rise up and drown us because there wasn't anything we could do about it. Or at least there wasn't anything we wanted to do about it: drowning was certainly better than crawling out from under the wet tent and floundering blindly about in the nettles and mud until a panther devoured us.

As it turned out, the creek didn't rise enough to pose any threat, and as incredible as it seems in retrospect, Rob and I actually fell asleep in the middle of our wet misery and awoke hours later to the sump-pump sound of a bittern greeting the dawn. Wordlessly, we gathered up most of the gear and began the long trek out of the swamp. We were soaking wet and covered with mud and mosquito bites and nettle blisters, and it was a very long struggle to get up the hill and through the Wicker briars and finally across the fence and into the Anderson pasture.

And there were the Anderson cows staring at us and waiting in the misty dawn for someone to come and get them for the morning milking. Rob looked at the cows, and then he walked over to a yellow and white Guernsey with a nose as big as a football.

"Hello, Fannie," Rob said, and put his arms around the cow's neck.

In other circumstances, that might have been an odd thing for my fishing pal to do. But I understood, and if I had known the cows personally I would have hugged one of them too.

It had been a great fishing trip. We hadn't caught any fish—we hadn't even fished—but we had survived, together, just the two of us, and that was the important thing, the kind of thing that can happen only between first fishing friends.

So Rob was the best there was, and though I have a clear sense of why he embraced the cow, I am still having a little trouble with the way he left me with the worms and went off to see Delores. And never mind that he ended up marrying her and fathering three lovely daughters. The obvious message here is that in the case of first-fishing-friends it is best if they can somehow synchronize their puberty.

THE CREED OF GREED

LONG BEFORE I BECAME one of them, people who used flies to catch trout were the "enemy." It was only a temporary circumstance, and I look back on it now as having very little to do with competing methods of catching trout and more to do with the universal inclination to be protective of favorite fishing spots. Greed is the bare hook here, and the brutal truth is that if there is an angler alive who graciously invites the multitudes to secret pools and runs, that angler desperately needs therapy. On the other hand, some kinds of selfish behavior smell like ripe fish.

Wayne Yureko knew all of this, and he passed some of it along during one of my adolescent summers as we fished the sparkling waters of the Clam River.

It began on a day that celebrated itself with soft breezes and spectacular sunshine. It was too bright for "wormers," which is what Wayne and I were, but Wayne, it seemed, could catch trout no matter the weather.

We separated at the bridge—Wayne headed downstream and I went upstream—and while it might not have been an ideal day for catching trout, it was so perfect in all other respects that I was infused with a kind of fishing euphoria.

Then suddenly the flawless fishing day turned dark and menacing as I stood knee-deep in the river and looked up at a scowling stranger on the bank. The man—as hard-eyed as a hawk—held a shiny, curve-bladed weed cutter, and while I knew that the scimitarlike tool was certainly not intended for beheading, that is what came immediately to mind.

"You can't fish here," the man said, his scowl deepening. "This is private."

I stared at him in sudden confusion and fright. A boy wrestling with the demons of puberty is on intimate terms with retreat, and when the blade-wielding man gestured downstream with his weed cutter and said, "Get out of here and don't come back!" I got!

The force of the river pushed on my legs and I stumbled on the slippery rocks, glancing back once to see the man watching me, his free hand shading his scowl, and his slouched posture as threatening as a sow bear's.

I headed downstream, hoping to see Wayne around the next bend, but knowing that he was a long way off, and furthermore he obviously wouldn't want his fishing interrupted by a spooked kid.

I don't know what there was about Wayne that made me think he was a lonely man. He was certainly cheerful most of the time, more so, perhaps when he cozied up to a shady country bar with a cold bottle of beer to celebrate one of our trout outings. He was a tall man, straight and strong, and his face and arms were tanned a leathery brown from years of working as a section hand on the Soo Line railroad. It was obviously hard, heavy work, and in its isolation it might have been lonely too. Wayne was a bachelor, and while that might have contributed to my perception of him as a lonely man, it gave him a lot of time for trout fishing.

It is possible that Wayne invited me to go fishing with him just to have company, but I doubt it. What kind of company is a skinny, doubt-ridden teenager? And then there was my recent egregious breach of fishing etiquette that certainly gave Wayne reason to ignore me. It had happened earlier in the season after Wayne had led me through a patch of thick woods to a hidden beaver pond on Benson Creek. In the sprawling dark water beneath the green duckweed of that pond there had been a fantastic population of the most beautiful brook trout imaginable—glistening black backs, white fins, and brilliant spots. And there seemed to be an inexhaustible supply of them, many twelve to fourteen inches long, and so bright orange–fleshed that their beauty continued on to the dinner table like a banner.

In what can only be blamed on a serious character flaw, I subsequently enlisted an older cousin who had a driver's license and a rattling old Ford, and we went to the hidden pond. He, in turn, took some of his brothers along, and then there were other friends, and . . .

Wayne never said anything about it, but he didn't have to. When he and I went to the pond, he saw the signs left by an ever growing crowd of fishermen, and he knew what had happened as certainly as I came to know that I had seriously violated a trust. Some of the things that you learn by osmosis go bone-deep and leave an ache, and for a while I was embarrassed to be in Wayne's presence. Not so much, however, that I refused his invitations to go fishing.

Some of this went through my mind that day on the Clam as I headed back to the car. And somehow in my retreat I had the feeling that I was failing yet another test of fishing character.

I knew it would be hours before Wayne showed up, so I fished the runs and slicks that he had already fished, using the telescoping steel rod to drift a night crawler, and watching the small brown trout dart for cover. But my heart was not in it: the confrontation had taken too much of a toll.

On the way home when Wayne stopped for his ritualistic beer, I told him what had happened. He muttered a curse and his beer bottle banged down so hard that condensation flew from it in a glistening shower, and the bartender jerked out of his semisnooze like a startled cat.

"Private!" Wayne roared. "Well, we'll just see about that," and he downed his beer with a series of loud glugs and ordered another.

"The laws are different in every state," Wayne said, "but here in Wisconsin they say that you can canoe or wade any stream that will float a log, and that includes the Clam River."

He sat quietly for a time and then he said, "There's a fishing club from the city where the guy chased you off. Maybe they think they own the river."

On the drive home, Wayne glanced over at me and said, "We'll go back to the Clam tomorrow and check this thing out."

And so we did, pulling on our boots the following morning and sloshing upstream through the sparkling rapids. As we approached the location of yesterday's encounter, Wayne stopped and motioned for me to go on ahead.

I waded around a bend, and was startled to find myself almost face-to-face with the man who had chased me off. Now instead of carrying a weed cutter, he was wielding a fly rod. He stopped in mid-cast as he saw me, and his line tangled in the alder tops.

"What the hell are you doing here?" he shouted. "I thought I told you to get out and stay out."

He moved toward me as he spoke, and then he stopped suddenly as Wayne splashed into view.

"Nice day," Wayne said, smiling and looking up at the fleecy clouds.

There were a few seconds of silence and then the man with the fly rod said, "This is private water. You can't fish here."

"Is that so," Wayne said. "Well, we don't think there is such a thing as private water in a free-flowing Wisconsin river."

As he spoke, Wayne swung his rod in such a way that the big night crawler on his hook plopped into the run that the fly fisherman had been working.

"Normally I would not crowd another fisherman like this," Wayne said, "but I can't get out on this private land to walk around you."

"I'm calling the sheriff," the man said.

"Good idea," Wayne said. "He'll explain the law to you. And by the way, we are planning to do a lot of fishing here."

"We'll see about that!" the man said as he turned and climbed out of the stream.

Wayne grinned at me, and then slowly the suspicion grew that this day had some special significance for a puberty-stricken boy who forever fancied himself victimized by the incessant prohibitions of society. I grinned back at Wayne as we slowly fished our way upstream.

We never saw anything of the sheriff, of course, and on subsequent trips to the Clam we were not bothered by anyone. And though I sometimes had the uneasy feeling that we were being watched, there was a special excitement in fishing up through the "private" property. I suppose in some strange way, Wayne had made it possible for me to feel a little like the gawky young bird that stumbles to the edge of the nest to exercise its wings for the first time.

As an adult, I lost touch with Wayne. But I thought about him often over the years, particularly when it was necessary to point out public wading and fishing rights to a cantankerous landowner. And I regret that I never got back home to buy Wayne a cold beer and to tell him how much I appreciated those early trout fishing trips.

Wayne died some years ago. His sister Phyllis, who lived with him, said he had planned to go fishing in the morning. He had his gear all ready, she said, but he died in his sleep.

Wayne would have made a joke out of that—something to obscure the ultimate loneliness, imagined or otherwise—and I can hear him saying, "I'd rather have gone fishing."

TROUT OR COWS

THERE ARE TIMES when work and trout fishing clash in an awesome rip tide of responsibility and guilt. Then you need someone like Carl Rowland to set things straight.

Carl was a quiet man of small, slightly stooped stature and slow, deliberate movement, and he obviously knew that in its pure form, the work ethic is a scourge and a pestilence. The only job Carl had during the years that I knew him was racking balls at the old poolhall, which meant that most of the time he sat on a bench and watched the pool players. And if he felt like going fishing, he simply walked out the back door and the pool players were on their own. It was a job that some people felt suited Carl's ambition. He was, in their opinion, easy-going onto lazy. But they were the workaholic sorts who thought it was a badge of honor to be painfully crippled from years of heavy lifting.

If you wanted to brood and you didn't want to do it alone, Carl was good company. He had an easy, sympathetic smile, and he was so sparing with his words that a conversation with him was mostly white space. This left plenty of opportunity for self-pitying introspection.

So on an early summer afternoon, I sat next to Carl back in the cavernous rear of the poolhall, inhaling the stale smell of strong tobacco and spilled beer and feeling sorry for myself. Like a yearling deer that must fend for itself when the new fawns are dropped, I had been shucked out of one of society's comfortable structures—high school—and had no clear idea what to do about my future. If anyone had tried to tell me that you had to plan your life—and I'm sure that my parents did—I had not been listening. The only thing I knew for sure was that I hated farm work with a passion, and it seemed to hate me in return. Just recently one of my father's cows had used a long, surprisingly limber hind leg to send me sprawling into a filthy gutter just because a fishhook in my hat accidentally pricked her flank as I leaned into her in the intimate posture of milking.

But farm work seemed to be my destiny and I was apparently powerless to do anything about it. That filled me with such an overwhelming sense of sadness that I felt as if I had been kicked in the stomach (by a cow!) and would never recover. The following evening—in time to help milk the cows—I was to start my first job as a hired hand on the Oscar Degerman farm. From the excitement and self-importance of graduating from high school, I was sinking into the sweaty, smelly job of tending to the orifices of indifferent beasts. My life, it seemed, had peaked out before it really started, and I was devastated.

I mentioned my impending job to Carl, adding that I was not looking forward to the dead-end drudgery of it. True to his stoicism and economy with words, he waited a long time before saying that the Degermans were "good people."

I agreed, and after another extended silence Carl said, "Hard workers too."

This sank me even deeper into my funk as I envisioned endless days of wrestling hay bales and wading through manure while shackled to the twice daily milking ritual.

There was another long stretch of silence—the better part of the afternoon, actually—and then Carl said, "Let's go fish the McKenzie tomorrow."

"I've got to be back in the evening to help milk Degerman's cows," I said, and Carl nodded.

We headed for McKenzie Creek before daylight the next morning, winding our way through the dew-drenched mix of Wisconsin woods and farms as daylight came creeping up out of the deep shadows. It was one of those quiet, breathless mornings, tentative and authoritative at the same time, and we rode through it in my old Chevrolet like reviewing royalty. Carl didn't say anything and neither did I. But in our silence we communicated. We were going fishing and we were both obviously happy with that: what was there to say?

I thought once about asking Carl to tell me about the time he caught three brown trout that were so big they covered the bottom of a washtub, but I didn't. I had heard about those fish from my father, who had known Carl since they were both kids. Dad liked to tell the story of how, when they were young men, it took Carl and a friend all summer to shingle the house because they spent so much time fishing. Carl and his pal would spend most of the night stalking browns along the Yellow River and then they would sleep most of the day, Dad said. But they caught lots of fish, and there was that time when they got those three huge brown trout. "Never saw such fish," Dad would say in telling the story. "Big as damn pigs."

Once off the gravel roads, there was a long drive on a narrow, rutted logging trail to get back to the McKenzie. As we traveled its tunnellike twists there was the vague sensation of leaving behind the cares and woes of the workaday world and entering into another dimension where it was all a thousand shades of sun-washed green and blue sky and timeless pleasure.

As we bounced through a mud hole, I think Carl said something about how nice it was to get into the woods, but I couldn't be sure. When he did talk he spoke so softly that it was very hard to hear him. If he was smiling when I looked at him, I nodded and smiled back, and words did not seem necessary.

We arrived at the grassy little clearing at the end of the trail and sat for a few seconds to soak up the special ambiance that always marks those first moments of arrival at a trout stream.

I went downstream and Carl went up, agreeing that we would meet back at the car for lunch. It was a beautiful day in the wilderness trout valley, and as it warmed to the rising sun, the buzz of insect and bird life became a hypnotic mantra. Time seemed as clear and clean as the creek water, and it passed with equal briskness. There were three medium-sized trout in the grass-lined creel when I looked at my watch and was surprised to see that it was past noon.

There was no sign of Carl back at the car. I called and when he didn't show up I started upstream to look for him. A deer trail wound through the white pine for a quarter of a mile, and then I saw Carl standing on the high bank. He turned his head slightly and motioned for silence as I eased up behind him.

"Look at the size of him!" he said, pointing down at the stream.

"Where?" I said.

"Right there. Must weigh eight pounds."

"What is it?"

"A trout. A big ol' brown."

I shaded my eyes and peered down into the roiling, sunwashed water.

"He knows we're here," Carl said.

"I don't see . . . " but even as I said it, the patterns of light seemed to freeze for a second and I caught the briefest outline of something big and torpedolike down in the depths of the hole. I couldn't believe a little stream like the McKenzie could hold such a big trout, and I suggested to Carl that we were looking at a tree root.

"It's a trout," he said. "We could get him tonight."

Tonight! We couldn't fish "tonight." I had to get to my new job. I had my mouth open to say as much but closed it without speaking. Carl glanced upstream and said, "He'll come up onto that mud flat when it gets dark. You can take him with chub tail."

I stared down at the trout, and suddenly the approaching summer of prickly hay bales and sweaty cows lay before me like an impossible quagmire.

Through the long, lazy afternoon of lounging about and fishing, I did my best not to think about Oscar Degerman's hay fields or his cows or anything else that had to do with work. It was the only way to keep guilt at bay, and the challenge to concentrate on the day at hand gave that afternoon a peculiar poignancy and clarity. There are, in fact, incidental details of it that still flash as bright as summer lightning: a cluster of bleached deer bones beside a hummock, a grouse that drummed so close by you could almost feel the concussion of air in its wings, and a circling hawk that screamed overhead. Carl napped for a while, and I spent most of the time wandering up and down the creek bottom, catching an occasional small trout and struggling mightily to evade the pantherlike stalking of a relentless conscience.

Finally then there was the darkness, like a warm cloak pulled slowly over the creek bottom. As the first stars winked down through the trees we began our pursuit, easing into position like a couple of night herons. It was very quiet, ominously so, it seemed, and the anticipation and excitement were so intense I would have exploded if there had been so much as a frog squeak. Then Carl clutched my arm and whispered for me to toss out the bait. The chunk of chub tail landed with a soft plunk, and I could feel goose bumps growing like pinfeathers.

It was so dark that I could not see the fish line, or even the stream itself. Then slowly the line tightened, and I could feel it moving downstream. It seemed to be going faster than the current, and Carl said, "He took it."

I let out an involuntary whoop and hauled back on the rod. The power of the fish came up through the tackle and into my shoulders like the snapping tether of a runaway horse. I had never felt anything like it in a trout and I pulled back so hard that I yanked the hook out of the fish's mouth.

And then, in the quiet of the night, I stood so filled with the adrenaline rush that there was no room for guilt.

"Damn," Carl said.

There were a few tense moments the next day with the family, talk about responsibility and that kind of thing. And when I went over to apologize, Oscar Degerman said maybe it would be better if he hired someone else. He didn't say as much, but I was sure he meant someone faithful to the dictum that in a rural community cows come before trout, always.

Then, unexpectedly, along came a job working in Cliff Horstman's service station where you tended to the orifices of machines instead of animals, which I thought was a higher calling. It wasn't, of course, but Cliff was a fisherman and we split up the work so it was possible to go fishing some part of every single day. What a job! I've never had one like it since.

Carl stopped down at the service station a week or so after I started my new job. We sat out by the gas pumps, mostly in silence, and finally Carl said, "Big trout, wasn't it?"

I nodded, and the quiet settled over us again.

SHOOT AND RELEASE

I NEVER BLAMED Uncle Charlie for what happened that day on the Couderay flowage. It was an accident . . . I think. But it would have been interesting to know just how big that musky was. And I have never been able to figure out if Uncle Charlie really wanted to know too, or if the musky was more valuable to him as a phantomlike monster that would forever defy man and measurement, perhaps as Nessie is to the people around Loch Ness. Was Uncle Charlie, in fact, practicing his own kind of perverse catch and release?

Uncle Charlie was not really my uncle. He was my mother's uncle, but everyone called him Uncle Charlie. He was an older man by the time I came along, and from the first time I saw him I was fascinated by the craggy, outdoor look of him and by the smell of gun oil and dried pelts that always preceded him and advertised the fact that when he wasn't guiding musky fishermen, he was a gun trader and a fur buyer. In my youthful mind this put him in a class with Daniel Boone and Davy Crockett, and it was a long time before I could relate to him with anything but slack-jawed adulation.

Uncle Charlie spent a lot of time around the little crossroads town of Radisson where one of his daughters lived and where his sister, Martha Helsing, and her family operated Helsing's Tavern. Radisson, in northwest Wisconsin, is on the edge of the Chequamegon National Forest, not far from the confluence of the Chippewa and Couderay rivers, which puts it close to some of the world's best musky water. A record musky—sixty-nine pounds, eleven ounces—was taken out of the Chippewa flowage back in 1949 by Louie Spray fishing off a sand bar just a twenty-minute drive from Radisson.

But Uncle Charlie's water was the Couderay flowage, a small impoundment that had sprawled over some of the rocky land and boggy marshes when a dam was put across the Couderay River. And he knew it well, down to the location of every sunken log and all of the deep holes that had been old gravel pits before the dam went in.

Like many musky guides of his era, Uncle Charlie used a revolver to dispatch big fish before bringing them into the boat, and when his gun—a .32 caliber Smith and Wesson—was not in the bottom of his tackle box, it was in one of his coat pockets. He seemed, in fact, to have developed a gunfighterlike attachment to the handgun, taking it with him even on the rare burial/baptism occasions when he made it to church. The revolver put a sag in the right-hand pocket of his old brown overcoat as he sat slouched in a rear pew, and since he kept the revolver well lubricated it strengthened the faint, sweet smell of gun oil that hung about him and which was not offensive in a rural community where animal smells invaded virtually every aspect of life, including the churches. There was, it seemed to me, much more prestige in smelling like a gun rather than a cow, economics notwithstanding. A game warden once asked Uncle Charlie why he carried the revolver and Uncle Charlie, a Norwegian, said, "Well, you never know when you might run into a Swede."

When I finally got old enough to finagle a musky fishing trip with Uncle Charlie he was, to put it kindly, in the twilight of his guiding prowess. Arthritis had put permanent crimps in his rowing arms and there was a little osteoporosis hump to his spine, as if his long outdoor years had transformed themselves into an uncomfortable little backpack. But Charlie was not ready for life's inevitable grand portage. Not by a long shot. He might have grunted and groaned a little over the effort of getting into the boat, but he wasn't about to let anyone else do the rowing, and he hadn't forgotten a detail of the river's underwater character nor any of the musky haunts.

The day that I went out with him was soft and gray, the kind that was good for musky fishing, according to Uncle Charlie, and as he rowed us away from shore he announced that we were going to have some action.

"Might even raise the big one," he said.

A giant musky was known to haunt the Couderay flowage, and over the years it had periodically terrorized innocent fishermen by smashing their tackle and occasionally surfacing like a whale so close to a boat that the occupants could look deep into the fish's hard, black eyes. Such experiences were always good for business up at Helsing's Tavern where the respective fishermen would retreat to restore their shattered nerves.

We were halfway around the flowage, gliding slowly past a rock outcrop to the rhythmic squeak of the oarlocks, when my bobber suddenly disappeared.

"Could be the big one," Uncle Charlie said. "He hangs out here sometimes."

I could feel my heart start to pound, erratically, like a rat trying desperately to leap out of an empty garbage can. I had never caught a muskie, and I had no idea what to expect.

"You might as well put down your rod and relax," Uncle Charlie said, stroking the oars gently to hold the boat in place. "It takes a musky at least half an hour to turn a sucker and swallow it."

It was very quiet, just the distant buzz of an engine somewhere off toward Radisson, and the vacant cawing of a crow. Time stopped and then went backward. I wanted to ask Uncle Charlie a hundred questions but that would only have emphasized the extent of my amateur standing. This was no time for that.

Uncle Charlie smoked a cigarette, and he seemed to be as calm as a bluegill fisherman.

I reached down for the fishing rod, and Uncle Charlie said, "Not yet. It's only been fifteen minutes."

Fifteen minutes, hell! It had been fifteen hours!

Finally, Uncle Charlie told me to pick up the rod and slowly reel the slack out of the line. Then the line was taunt, and Uncle Charlie said, "NOW!"

I brought the rod back with all my strength and the line snapped tight.

"HIT HIM AGAIN! HIT HIM AGAIN!" Uncle Charlie shouted.

I hauled back on the rod a second time, and then way out where the bobber had disappeared, the water erupted in a volcanic explosion around a giant fish that hung over the shattered surface for just a second before splashing back beneath the radiating circles of water.

The size of the fish and its violent appearance pretty much destroyed me, shattering any capacity for calculated activity and seriously damaging even basic reflexes. Uncle Charlie was shouting but I couldn't make out what he was saying as I waved the rod around and turned the reel handle backward so that a big tangle of line developed.

The fish leaped again and out of the corner of my eye I saw that Uncle Charlie had his revolver out and was shooting at the fish. I could hear the sharp snap of the gun and see where the bullets splatted against the water. Then without warning, the line suddenly broke and I nearly tumbled out of the boat.

"He broke off," Uncle Charlie said finally.

"But . . . "

"You should've given him some line."

I wanted to ask Uncle Charlie why he had been shooting at the fish before it was anywhere near the boat, but I kept my mouth shut and reeled in the line. It was, of course, not likely that it had been severed by a bullet, but I had my suspicions.

We didn't fish much after that. Uncle Charlie seemed to have lost his zest for it and I was emotionally drained and ready to call it a day. As we gathered up the gear and stowed the boat it seemed to me that Uncle Charlie was unusually cheerful for a man who had just been party to losing what could have been a record fish.

"You're young," he said, apparently sensing my disappointment. "You'll get more chances at the big ones."

And then he took the revolver out of his tackle box and slipped it into a coat pocket as we headed up toward Helsing's Tavern.

RAINBOW'S END

IT IS THE PRIVILEGE and obligation of anglers to act the fool at every opportunity. The rest of society expects it of us, and deep down we even expect it of ourselves. Trout fishing is, of course, the "A" number-one exhibit: hordes of evolution's "grandest" primate whipping incredibly expensive gear at the air and water with the seriousness of surgeons as they try to convince small-brained aquatic life forms that bits of feathers and hair are insects. Flavor the scene with thousands of bloodthirsty mosquitoes, throw in constantly tangled tackle, as well as pratfalls in black muck and cold water; and imbue the participant with a peculiar inclination to embellish and romanticize.

I rest my case.

This verity about obligatory lunacy was not obvious to me, however, the day that Uncle Earl and I did such a great job of making fools of ourselves with the hatchery trout.

Had I known about fishing's intimacy with outrageousness, I might not have taken it all so seriously, and might even have continued to woo Ed Meyers's dark-eyed daughter. It was my feeling at the time, however, that you cannot court a girl whose father views you as a lying nincompoop. (This was obviously long before I experienced a courting-age daughter of my own.)

Uncle Earl was one of those fortunate, cheerful people with a facility for seizing the moment. That made it easy for him to hop down off an old Farmall tractor and accept my invitation to try for the big bluegills in Granite Lake.

"More fun than cultivating corn," Earl said, and away we went.

Earl was a sinewy man with gray, twinkling eyes and a hair-trigger, staccato laugh. "Fine day for fishing," he said as he fired up his pipe and exhaled clouds of smoke strong enough to knock birds out of the sky.

It was indeed a fine day for fishing—sunny, warm, and with a soft breeze brushing the lake's surface as we pulled into the Granite Lake parking lot. We baited up with night crawlers and used long bamboo poles to swing the hooks and bobbers out beyond the lily pads.

But the bluegills were not biting, and the bobbers were as motionless as sticks in mud. We sat with our backs against a log and stretched our legs out over the warm sand, and a significant relaxed state set in.

Earl mumbled something about how important it was not to work on such a fine day, and in our stuporous repose, we didn't pay much attention to the truck that pulled into the parking lot and stopped behind a cluster of trees. Minutes later, however, I casually opened one eye to see my bobber sink slowly beneath the surface. I heaved back on the fish pole, expecting a bluegill to come corkscrewing up in a cascade of water. Instead, the pole bent into a dangerous U as the line snapped tight enough to slice cheese.

I hung on, and then in a spray of sparkling droplets, a rainbow trout burst through the surface. I couldn't believe it, and as I brought the fish to land and stood admiring its sleek fifteen-inch contours, I saw from the corner of my eye that Earl was up on his feet and struggling with a fish.

"OOOOOOeeeeeeee," Earl shouted. "What have we got us here!"

"Trout," I shouted. "Rainbow trout."

"Where the hell did they come from?" Earl said as he pulled in his fish and held it up in amazement.

"Can you believe this?" I said, but Earl did not answer. He was too busy tugging at another fish, a big fish that he quickly horsed up onto the sand at his feet. It was a huge rainbow, at least three pounds.

"I'll be damned," Earl said, looking down at the trophy-size fish. "Good lookin' trout, but they don't have much fight to 'em."

Earl was right. While the rainbows were pretty to look at, they were strangely lethargic on the end of the line. As trout went, they were nothing like the scrappy little Engle Creek brookies we were accustomed to.

We put Earl's big trout on a stringer with the others, tied the stringer to an alder, and went back to fishing, the meat-fishing mentality of the time engulfing us like a fever. Almost at once we were hooked to two more fish, smaller than Earl's trophy, but much bigger trout than we usually caught. It went on like that until we had a stringer full.

"How the hell did rainbows get into Granite Lake?" Earl said as we counted to make sure we were not over our collective twenty-fish limit.

An explanation came almost immediately in the form of Game Warden Jim Scolman, who was suddenly standing between Earl and me. We had not seen him approach, and his sudden, scowling appearance startled us.

"Nice fish, huh," the warden said.

"Hogs," Earl said. "Fat hogs."

"They're surplus hatchery stock," Scolman said. "We just planted 'em."

Earl glanced through the trees to where the Conservation Department truck was parked. "I'll be!" he said. "Government workers. These trout are government workers, Billy. No wonder they got no pep."

Warden Scolman gave Earl a quick look, and said, "They won't be very good eating until they've been in the lake for a while."

"They don't fight and you can't eat 'em; what the hell good are they?" Earl said, and laughed his machine-gun laugh.

"I guess they're just show-off fish," Scolman said. "We put them in here mostly for the kids."

Earl looked over at the stringer and said, "Let's turn 'em loose. No sense keeping fish we can't eat."

But it was too late. The stress of their truck ride or the strain of being caught and held on the stringer had apparently been too much for the trout and they had all turned belly-up.

"Might as well take 'em home," Earl said. "Maybe try that old recipe where you cook a fish on a board and then eat the board."

As we left the lake, Earl exhaled a cloud of foul pipe smoke, and said, "Did you hear the warden call those trout 'show-off fish'?"

"Yeah," I said.

"Well, just for fun, let's go to town and show 'em off a little."

And that is what we did. Except we didn't show them off a little; we showed them off a lot. We stopped first at the poolhall and Earl carried in the stringer of dead rainbows and flopped it down on the bar as if he were delivering salvation.

"Where the hell did you catch those?" proprietor Niles Hoover shouted as the regulars slid off their stools and swung away from the card tables to gather around.

"Secret place," Earl said.

I stared at him in surprise, and he grinned back. The men looked at the trout and at Earl, and a few of them glanced over at me as I nodded agreement, quickly anxious to be a part of Earl's intriguing fabrication.

"Might be some old lumber baron's lost trout pond." Earl said. "It's so far back in we may not be able to find it again ourselves."

From the poolhall we went to several service stations, the feed mill, the hardware store, and the lumberyard. At each stop we basked in the adulation of admirers, and added bits and pieces to the impromptu "lost pond" story. And each time it was repeated it sounded better, so much so, in fact, that in a way I began to believe it myself. If we didn't actually use the name of Granite Lake in our story, didn't that mean that it was somehow "lost"?

The lumberyard, where Ed Meyers was the manager, was an important stop for me because Ed's daughter Patricia was the current object of my youthful yearning. And it was a significant yearn, complete with stumbling speechlessness in Patricia's presence and lust-filled dreams about what could be. Patricia was not at the lumberyard, of course, but her father—a trout fisherman—looked at the rainbows and then at Earl and me and said, "Never saw anything like it. Where'd you catch them?"

"Secret place," I said. "Way back in the brush."

I was hoping, of course, that Ed would pass on the word to his daughter that I was a terrific fisherman, and henceforth an upstanding young man worthy of her attention.

Earl and I went home, finally, and though our respective families made valiant efforts to eat the rainbows, most of the fish went to the cats or ended up buried behind the barn. The rainbows' doubtful palatability had obviously not been improved by our having dragged them around town so long that they began to dry out and attract flies.

And then several days later the weekly issue of the Barron County News Shield printed a news release from the Conservation Department. A strange little chill went up my spine when I read the headline: "Surplus Rainbows Planted in Granite Lake."

The news release said that the trout would be very vulnerable and easily caught until they became acclimated to the lake, and it suggested that only children fish for them.

I had been destroyed!

It went beyond humiliation and, of course, meant that I would never again be able to face Ed Meyers or his daughter.

The members of my immediate family didn't seem to recognize the seriousness of what had happened, in particular my younger brother Orv who grinned and asked me to take him fishing, "where you and Uncle Earl caught all the trout."

In fact, everyone tended to dismiss the incident as a big joke. Even Uncle Earl, who visited one day and said he had just come from the poolhall where they had razzed him something awful. And then he had laughed until I wanted to hit him in the mouth.

In retrospect, I know I should have been able to laugh along with Earl and the others. But we are not born with the knowledge that fishermen are obligated to make fools of themselves. It is something we have to learn, like how much it hurts when the wind whips a weighted No. 4 nymph so that it impales itself in the gristly part of your ear, or how when you forget to replace the drain plug the boat will sink while you are parking the trailer, or how night crawlers tipped over in the trunk can crawl under the floor mats to make an expensive car unusable, or . . .

But I learned something from the experience. I vowed that I would never again embellish another fish story. Never. Ever. Which, of course, has turned out to be the biggest embellishment of all.

THE WEASEL

JUST HOW GOING off to war advances the cause of trout fishing is not clear. But in the male trout fisher's nymphal stage—just before testosterone comes to a rolling boil—he sees opportunity in war, a chance to prove to himself and the world that he is ready to compete with the old bucks for a chance at the herd.

It is a ludicrous assessment that leaves the young men either dead or disappointed. It keeps repeating itself, however, like a cultural plague, and it made my teenage years miserable because I was too young for the glories of the big war. Then came Korea. I couldn't wait to get shot at.

This absurdity was reinforced by the fact that one of my role models at the time was Rollin (R. B.) Curtis, one of the most decorated soldiers of World War One. Rollin's personal heroics during that gaseous little Gary Cooper "Over There" war-to-end-all-wars had earned him a French medal and a lot of U.S. medals, and he had some war-related disability so he got a small pension. Rollin did not talk much about the war. In fact, the only thing he ever told me about it was how a little terrier ran around a French battlefield biting at the puffs of dust where bullets hit.

"It was the damnedest thing," he said, and then he laughed that laugh of his, that booming, whooping, head-thrown-back, eyes closed, mouth-open, tongue-glistening laugh that filled a room or a car and bounced against your ears like a drum beat; and you knew that the man who produced it was really into it—was laughing with such abandon that he wasn't thinking about anything, just laughing. Then the only thing you could do was join in, not thinking about anything either.

Rollin never said what he or anybody else was doing when the terrier was biting at the bullets. But you could imagine the shadowy images of young men in ridiculous soup-bowl helmets and khaki knickers hiding behind hedges with old bolt-action rifles held at port arms, watching the little dog and then running across the dusty field themselves and diving into trenches, or falling as if they had bitten one of the bullets.

Rollin was great company for a kid who felt left out of the ultimate excitement of the time. He had been there and he had done that, and he didn't mind a little restrained adulation. And he loved to fish for trout. I don't know if I really learned anything from Rollin about war, but I did learn from him that if you stand too long in a frigid trout stream, your privates will disappear up into your body with the force of slow-moving bullets. A trout fisherman needs to be aware of that, Rollin said, and to recognize that while it is simply nature's way of protecting a species against its own perversity, it should not be overdone.

One cold spring day we headed for the Flag River for a little reminder of this verity. Rollin and some of his friends had a fishing shack in a backwoods stand of poplar and spruce near the river, and he said he wanted to show it to me. I was anxious to see it, of course, because it was yet another place that Rollin knew and I didn't.

We drove north—Rollin's hawk-nose profile like the Indian on the old buffalo nickel—on the highway that sliced straight through the woods as if it had been laid down by a whip, and we passed the leading edge of spring somewhere down around the village of Minong. The deep snow was gone, but you could feel in the chill of the air that it hadn't been gone long, and that it had retreated reluctantly. At some point we crossed over the divide where the streams flow north into Lake Superior instead of south into the Mississippi. The Flag is one of those northbound streams and its waters must curse the fate of never getting warm in a land of mud and magnolias. Instead, it tumbles north in a series of cold rapids to join the frigid waters of Lake Superior at the little village of Port Wing.

There were no leaves on the trees yet—not even buds, in fact—and you could look into the woods and see its guts, its brown humus and downed trees and rotting stumps, the exquisite tangle and harmony of it; and you could feel the way it reached out to everything. And everywhere there were deer, like long-legged parasites meandering over a sodden old host that was about to heave itself up and throw them a party. They were in twos and threes and sometimes little herds and you could not look at a hill or a swamp without seeing them.

"Look at 'em!" Rollin said once as we rounded a bend and the white flags of deer went waving off the road and into the brush. "Get out of our way, you damn sheep," Rollin shouted, making a sweeping gesture with his arm and filling the car with his booming laugh.

Sometimes the deep snow of northern Wisconsin forces the deer to concentrate in thick cedar swamps, and then the brutal cold reaches deep down into their empty guts and kills them so that their curled corpses lie on the trails in neat rows, like strange punctuation for a brutal winter. But there hadn't been a winter like that for a few years and the deer had propagated explosively. In their proliferation they gave the bare woods a strange sense of motion as it emerged from the prison of winter.

The dead grass in front of the shack was crushed flat from the weight of the snow, and it was like a cushion beneath our feet as we got out of the car.

"There it is," Rollin said, waving a hand at the shack. "It's a beaut, ain't it."

And it was, in a forlorn, dilapidated way. In its fragile statement about man against the woods, it was indeed "a beaut," all weathered and unpainted and tarpaper shaggy and sinking down in a sagging crouch. We stood and looked at it, and Rollin shook his head and laughed.

A shadowy form moved across a corner of the cluttered room as we pushed through the shack's unlocked door and into its stale darkness. The movement stopped us short and we stood and blinked into the dimness, inhaling the dank, strong air that was full of earthy animal smells and the trapped, musty aromas of the past so that it came to your lungs like mold. Then there was another movement in the corner.

"A damn porky," Rollin whooped as he bent to grab up a broom from the debris on the floor.

"Get! Get outa here you pincushion," he shouted and stepped nimbly over to make sweeping motions at the porcupine.

The porcupine cowered in the corner, and Rollin looked down at it and laughed. "You poor bastard," he said.

We left the door open when we went fishing and the porcupine was gone when we got back. The fishing wasn't much. It was too cold and too early and the trout were tucked up under the red clay banks and still deep into their winter fasts. We waded a few pools and tossed muddler minnows and Rollin tried some worms but it wasn't any use and all we did was get cold and numb as we stumbled around on the smooth, slippery rocks and tried not to fall down. We quit fishing after Rollin made his usual little speech about how wading in such cold water could be overdone.

Back at the shack, we pulled shotguns out of the car trunk and took turns shooting at clay birds that we threw for each other. The targets sailed smoothly out over the spindly treetops, finally striking the slim branches and then skewing to the ground behind the boom of the gun. Rollin hit more targets than I did, and he would laugh with each hit as if it had given him tremendous pleasure.

It was my turn to shoot and I was waiting for Rollin to load the bird thrower when a weasel poked up suddenly out of the woodpile. It was pure white and it stood up phalluslike on a piece of rotting wood and peered at us.

"Take him," Rollin whispered, and I swung the shotgun, aimed down its barrel, and pulled the trigger. The charge blew the weasel's head off and its body flopped back off the chunk of wood.

"JEEEEzus," Rollin shouted. "What the hell did you do that for?"

"You told me to," I said.

"Well, goddamn, you shouldn't have done that."

A breeze sighed through the trees, the ebbing of the afternoon wind, and then it was still and quiet, a hush between episodes. Finally Rollin spoke, "Now we gotta eat the sunuvabitch," he said, and when I looked at him he suddenly threw back his head and laughed so loud that the sound of it echoed back from the distant ridge of trees.

We stopped at a tavern on the way home and Rollin said he would bet ten dollars that he could stand next to a bar stool and jump up onto it with both feet. I took the bet and lost, of course, and Rollin kept my ten dollars until the next day when he gave it back and said, "Never take another man's bet."

Nothing more was ever said about the weasel, but I could not shake the image of the tiny animal's headless body tumbling back among the sticks of wood, nor could I shake the sense of despair that sprouted up out of Rollin's chastisement.

It was not long after that trip to the Flag that I ended up in Korea on a hill that had been blasted by artillery from both sides for so long that it was just a big heap of splinters and dirt. From the slit between the logs of a battered observation post you could squint through the spotting scope and watch the North Koreans, except that you didn't see much of them because whenever they showed themselves we called down to the tanks and the field 90 and they shot the hell out of them, or those little star-shaped jets came in and dumped enough napalm to produce fireballs the size of thunderheads. Sometimes we went out on patrols and usually we didn't find anything, just rocks and old rice paddies and that ominous quiet that was cold and clammy on your skin. And sometimes there would be the little zing and snap of bullets that would flatten us to the ground and then we would crawl away like lizards.

I would think about Rollin sometimes. On a bright afternoon, when we all should have been back in the U.S. lolling on the grass of parks and campuses, or wading the clear, clean trout rivers, we climbed up the side of a steep hill, and suddenly bullets and mortars were landing all around and we turned and ran because we were scared out of our minds and because it was not our job to fight but only to establish contact. (We were the I and R platoon—Intelligence and Reconnaissance, the Army called us. Idiots and Retarded is how we saw it.) Mostly, of course, we ran down off the hill because we thought we were going to die, and when we finally stopped—two guys from the third squad didn't make it—and lay gasping on the smooth rocks in the bottom of a dry creek bed, I remembered the dust that had erupted up where the mortar shells and bullets hit, and I knew at that second that I would never be the same again.

But then we are never what we were a second ago. Electrical impulses and growth and degeneration rearrange cells, and recovery from passion or raw, raging fear or even a sneeze can never be complete. Lying on the rocks, I thought that I might never catch my breath again, not really; and it was as if I had been wading the Flag and my glandular identity was hopelessly lost somewhere up in the tangle of my insides. I dropped my head down and rested it on the smooth rocks, like the ones we had stumbled over in the cold water of the Flag.

And then I was suddenly so goddamn mad at laughing, old veteran R. B. Curtis that I wanted to kick his ass.

FLY FISHING DOG

AS ONE OF MY very best outdoor pals, Doc pretty much insisted on being involved in everything, and the fact that he was a springer spaniel did not seem to seriously handicap him as a dry fly fisherman (fisherdog?). He would react to rising trout with the same kind of crazed enthusiasm that many of his human friends exhibited. And his repeated failure from a catch standpoint never in the slightest dimmed his zeal, also a circumstance familiar to many two-legged trouters. Participation seemed to be the important thing.

Doc was, of course, supposed to earn his keep by flushing and occasionally even retrieving grouse and woodcock, and this he was willing to do on his terms, which included exercising the resident deer; either mating or fighting with other hunters' dogs; terrorizing farmyard poultry, innocent cows, and even an occasional pig; and quitting the swamp when he damn well felt like it. All of this probably says more about my shortcomings as a dog owner than I would care to admit. However, though I had paid for him as a pup, bought his dog food, saw to his vet bills, and paid angry farmers not to sue over a couple of chickens or a Muscovy duck or two, neither Doc nor I saw me as his "owner." I was more like his "man," in the way that a rich English squire has a "man" to tend to the routine and sometimes annoying details of daily life.

If Doc had been able to get a driver's license and been allowed to run at large so he could have scrounged in backyards and garbage cans for food, he would not have needed me. In fact, more often than not I seemed to come off as a hindrance to what he considered the full and rightful enjoyment of his canine existence.

I'm not sure just when Doc started dry fly fishing. All I know is that I looked out the cabin window one day to see him make a flying leap into the creek. He hit the water with his floppy ears flying and his mouth snapping at the surface, swam around briefly, and then hauled himself back onto the bank and stood staring at the stream. Seconds later he leaped in again, this time up by the bend where the elm tree hangs out over an under-cut bank. Again he landed with his jaws working, and after swimming in a tight circle, he was back on the bank.

"That damn dog is dry fly fishing," I said to John Lawton, my fishing companion, who was sitting up to the table with his waders on and eating fried trout and potatoes with his hands.

John watched as Doc continued his frenzied activity, alternately staring at the creek and then leaping in when he spotted a brook trout rise to take a caddis fly.

"He fishes like you do," John said. "Lots of waste motion but no fish."

"I caught your lunch, didn't I," I said, and turned to watch John suck the meat off a trout skeleton like a kid finishing a popsicle.

Earlier in the day, the lunch trout had gobbled a small Adams with uncommon enthusiasm, and as usual I had had to shut Doc in the cabin to keep him from charging up and down the stream bank and scaring all the fish. He hated this, of course, and he cursed me with his eyes as I tried to explain that he was a bird dog and not a fish dog.

He would watch me through the glass front of the cabin as I tromped down to the creek, and after a couple of snarling barks that could only be profanity of the worst kind, he would flop down and stare at me until I was out of sight.

Obviously he had watched me as I caught some of our lunch trout, and while there is no way to confirm it, I am convinced that he must have said to himself, "If that dumb bastard can catch trout, so can I."

And so he had tried it and obviously found it to his liking because from that day on he watched the creek like a heron, and when there were fish feeding on the surface he acted as crazy in his way as any fly rod devotee. I did not want my dog to fish, but there was nothing I could do about it, and it is interesting to speculate, anthropomorphically, on what the trout might have thought of Doc's fishing technique: "What the hell was that? Scared the bejesus out of me. Looked like a hair bomb!"

It is, of course, an unforgivable lapse to allow a dog to get out of control under any circumstance, and there is usually a price to pay when it happens. That was certainly the case when Doc got me into trouble with agents of the Federal government, and it was probably only because they were so anxious for both of us to get out of their sight that the incident did not accelerate into incarceration for Doc or me.

The setting was that portion of the Horicon Wildlife Refuge that is presided over by the U.S. Fish and Wildlife Service, and the time was way back when the game biologists were experimenting with hazing geese in an effort to get them to move along the migratory route and leave the smorgasbord of Wisconsin farmland. Among the goose-hazing devices were a strange-appearing swamp buggy that roared through the cattails behind erupting hordes of geese and a single-engine aircraft that buzzed the squawking flocks and tried to herd them in a southerly direction. The efforts were pretty much futile, rather like trying to chase kids out of a candy factory with a feather duster.

At one point on this particular autumn, Doc and I happened along the marsh, and I drove in to one of the parking lots to have a look at the breathtaking mass of birds. Doc, forever alert to opportunity for sport and suspicious that I might interfere, squirmed his way through the car door just as I cracked the latch, and while I made a grab for him, I was no match for his escape speed.

I shouted for him to "GET BACK HERE," but I might as well have been shouting at the moon. Doc ran in a kind of exploratory circle, and the nearest geese stopped feeding and stretched their necks to look at him. Doc looked back and obviously couldn't believe what he saw. Here were hundreds, no, tens of thousands of great big juicy-looking birds with the kind of long-necked arrogance that would motivate any self-respecting bird dog to put them in their place.

Doc promptly went about the job. He widened his exploratory circle until the nearest geese began to lift into the air, honking their objections and looking down at their flop-eared nemesis. Doc seemed to pick up speed and ran in still larger circles as hundreds and then thousands of geese took to the air in a wild cacophony of goose babble.

I added my shouting to the din, and even made a futile dash to try to intercept Doc on one of his circular routes. I got close enough only to see the saliva dripping from his lolling tongue and the glazed look in his eyes. He obviously thought he had gone to some kind of bird-dog heaven and been freed forever from the annoyance of my attempts to try to limit his fun.

It became a spectacle of no small dimensions—the sky literally filled with geese from horizon to horizon—and I finally gave up any attempts to stop it. I was standing in some awe of what Doc had wrought when a pickup truck with the Fish and Wildlife Service insignia on the door pulled up, stopping in a slight skid as a young man jumped out of the vehicle.

"What the hell are you doing," he said, sweeping his arm overhead to indicate the routed geese.

"Trying to catch my dog," I said.

"You should not have let him loose," the FWS agent said. "We've got rules against dogs harassing the birds."

My mind filled with visions of Doc and me being thrown into Federal lockups, and I took up my shouting at Doc.

It was apparent to the agent that it was a hopeless endeavor, and he leaned back against his pickup and watched the geese mill about overhead.

"We can't have dogs running all over the marsh," he said, but his voice had taken on a note of resignation.

We both stood there in silence then as Doc ran himself to exhaustion and began to slow down. Finally Doc headed back toward the car, and the agent said that if I would catch him and promise never to bring him back to the marsh he would not write us a ticket.

I resisted the impulse to suggest that Doc might be cheaper than the swamp buggy and the airplane for hazing geese. It is best not to rock a boat that is taking you out of troubled waters.

I cursed and lectured Doc on the way home, but he had fallen into a deep sleep on the back seat and never heard a thing.

One of my favorite brook trout streams slices across the back forty of a farmer friend named Frank who also liked to go along whenever Doc and I showed up during the grouse season. On one of those grouse hunting days, we were standing near the barn with our shotguns in the crooks of our arms and trying to locate Doc so we could start our hunt. I had been calling for him, and Frank suggested that maybe Doc was with his cow dog, which was a female and might be in heat.

"But I just got rid of one litter of pups and I don't want any more," Frank said emphatically.

Even as he spoke, out from behind the barn came Frank's dog, and in that awkward aftermath of canine sexual intercourse, Doc was hooked up to her like a trapped rat.

Frank raised his gun and said, "Which one of the sunzabitches should I shoot first?"

For just a fraction of a second, I thought Frank was serious, but then he lowered his shotgun and grinned.

If there is any circumstance that gives meaning to "compromising position" it must be that of the male dog who, having satisfied his lust, is then firmly attached to the object of his conquest. It must be not only painful but a condition of great mystery to the participants and—if the male dog's demeanor and expression can be used as a gauge—also one of abject humiliation. So Doc suffered through it all, and when we were finally able to head for the woods, he had no more enthusiasm for the hunt than a Teddy bear.

I scolded him, and Frank said, "Hey, save your breath, and hope that next time it is you who doesn't have energy left over for the hunt."

Once when Doc and I were floating the Westfield River on an exploratory spring trout trip, Doc tipped over the canoe when he made a sudden leap in the direction of a family of raccoons. Just why Doc was along baffles me now, but it was probably because of one of his unnegotiable demands, and my dereliction as a disciplinarian.

Around our neighborhood, Doc was appreciated for his general good humor, but he was also under suspicion much of the time for various misdeeds. He was supposed to be in his kennel or on a leash at all times, but if a family member was outside to watch him, the theory was that it would be okay to let him out in the yard. Doc would, of course, sneak off to see what he could find, and one afternoon he came home carrying the largest raw steak I have ever seen. Obviously somebody had been ready to do some backyard grilling and somehow Doc had made off with the meat.

Another time he slipped into a neighbor's garage and devoured several pans of cooling hors d'oeuvres that were intended for a graduation party.

And once . . . but this could go on and on, and perhaps to portray Doc as having the character of a typical fisherman, enough has been recorded.

To my knowledge, the only actual physical contact that Doc ever had with a fish was once when we were walking the shore of Lake Mendota and he ran ahead to find a dead and very rotten carp which he then proceeded to wallow in, rubbing the stench so deeply into his fur that he was not fit company for a skunk.

I can remember the stink to this day, and there are those who claim that the olfactory machinery has a better memory than the other senses. I don't know about that, because the image of Doc dry fly fishing down by the bridge is pretty sharp too.

And I can still hear those milling geese.

TROUT MYSTERY

THOUGH WE ARE now in the "tell all" age, which gives no more respect to any of the departed than you would give to a rock, something about the task at hand bothers me. However, I like to think I am driven by the relentless search for truth, which writers are forever using to excuse the machinations of their ego.

Also, it is just too much fun to contemplate what might have been if the web of evidence and suspicion had surfaced earlier.

In any case, as Bob Williams himself might have put it, "Tail with the hide."

Bob Williams was one of those people who could do anything and do it well, and that carried over to his trout fishing. He always seemed to make the right decisions about where and when to fish and which fly to use and how to deliver it.

To say that we were opposites is to put it kindly. I can't make a square cut with a saw to save my life, and if you want to know about new ways to screw up trout fishing, I'm your man.

So, these facts considered, we were an unlikely duo. Perhaps Bob saw my ineptness as a form of entertainment, or as a therapeutic way to vent emotion. Whenever I goofed at whatever we were involved in, Bob's voice would rise a couple of octaves and he would utter the familiar, "JEEEEEZUS KEEERIST, Stokes, what are you doing now!"

And when I was unable either to explain or to correct my actions, Bob would brusquely take charge, grabbing at whatever tools were involved or shouting impatient instructions in his voice of high-pitched indignation.

It went that way on the trout streams, until I would fish around a bend and out of his sight. I prefer solitary fishing, especially when it eliminates profane tutorial judgments that echo up a creek bottom like the yodeling of a sandhill crane. But I learned some things about trout fishing from Bob. He was big on using what he called "locators"—big hairy flies that he used both wet and dry to coax out big browns.

"They probably won't hit it, but they'll come out to see what the hell it is," he said. "Then you get 'em later with something on their menu."

And Bob taught me that if the right kind of hatch is on, you can catch trout in a downpour.

"The fish are already wet," he said. "They don't care that it is raining."

There were, in fact, not many circumstances under which Bob could not catch trout. We would separate on a stream after he had administered his quota of sputtering advice, and later when we were through fishing and got back together, he always had trout. There were days when I swear a stream would be so dead you couldn't have caught a shiner with a seine, and yet Bob would show up with trout.

Then it would be my turn to sputter, and Bob would laugh and make some remark like, "Small flies. Twenty-twos, fished with delicacy."

Without Bob's help, my Back-40 cabin never would have been built. Or if I had managed to put it together, it probably would have collapsed like a house of cards, or ended up looking like a stack of salvaged lumber.

Bob would show up at the Back-40 almost every weekend, arriving in a bluster of disapproval over whatever I was doing and greeting my young sons with great enthusiasm. They loved him, and especially so after one weekend when he decided that instead of working on the cabin, he was going to build them a tree house. It was one helluva tree house, high up in the gnarled branches of an oak that hung out over the creek, and complete with roof and a small stove to ward off the chill.

Almost every weekend for a year or so we would work at the cabin, and Bob would sometimes stop and curse at the occasional fisherman who wandered past. "Damn wormers," he would grumble, and then go back to his hammering. At some point every day, Bob would drop his hammer or saw and say, "That's it, Stokes. It's time to go fishin'."

Sometimes we fished the creek that ran past the front of the cabin, even though it was almost impossible to keep my springer spaniel, Doc, from suddenly showing up beside the pool you were trying to fish. Doc and Bob were good friends, and Doc did not understand why that friendship seemed to dissolve whenever he showed up to "help" Bob catch brook trout. You could hear Bob's complaints and curses, and finally he would come back to the cabin, with a chagrined Doc at his heels.

"Your dog is just like you, Stokes, nothin' but trouble," Bob would say.

Once the cabin was built, we expanded our fishing to take in such streams as the Wolf River, and it was on one such trip that Bob's indignation over my questionable judgment reached new heights.

We were headed up to the Wolf one pleasant summer day when I turned off twisting old Highway 52 and onto a logging road that twisted even more.

"Where the hell are you going?" Bob Williams said, his voice rising only slightly.

"Short cut," I said.

"Short cut!" he said, and his voice began that familiar creep up across the octaves.

"I checked it out on a map and I think it will take us down to the Oxbow."

"You think! YOU THINK!"

"I was in here once with John, but it was after dark and . . . "

"Stokes, you can't find your way home from the grocery store. You're gonna get us lost and probably stuck in some mud hole."

"If we're going to hit the evening hatch, we've got to get on the river as soon as possible."

"But you don't even know if this trail goes to the river."

"I'm pretty sure."

Bob shook his head in despair and slumped back against the car seat. "Where's the brandy?" he said.

I followed the winding trail until it forked off in two directions, and when I took the fork to the right, Bob said I should have gone left.

At about this point, my old Chevrolet's engine coughed once and then suddenly stopped. As we coasted to a halt, I glanced down at the gas gauge and saw that it registered empty. My god! I had meant to buy gas back in Antigo, and then it had slipped my mind. How could I have been so stupid? I sat and stared at the gas gauge in disbelief.

"Are we out of gas, Stokes?" Bob said, craning his neck to look at me, and settling his voice in an unusual low timbre.

When I did not respond, and the stillness of the woods came down over us, along with swarms of mosquitoes that obviously considered the open car windows to be the gates to a bloody heaven, Bob sat in uncharacteristic silence for a few seconds. I knew this was very temporary, however, and thought of him as a rooster gathering himself to break the peace of a quiet morning with outrageous noise.

Bob did not disappoint me. He began a tirade that laid out my stupidity along with the details of our dilemma—lost in the woods forty miles from nowhere, with night coming on and nothing but mosquitoes for company.

"Start walkin', Stokes," Bob said. "I'm stayin' here with the brandy."

There are no houses for miles along 52, and I sat there contemplating a walk that would take me halfway into the night.

"Get your ass in gear," Bob said, twisting the cork out of the bottle.

I was about to get out of the car and head back up the trail, when suddenly a battered pickup truck appeared over the rocky ridge in front of us. As we stared open-mouthed, it skidded to a stop and a trio of pulpwood cutters looked out at us.

"Stokes, you just came up smellin' like a rose," Bob said. "I can't believe it."

The loggers had a gas tank in the box of their truck and when one of them pointed at a siphon hose, Bob grabbed it and shoved it into my face. "Suck, Stokes, goddamnit, suck."

When we had transferred enough gas to get us out of the woods, Bob gave the loggers the brandy and all the beer we had along and ordered me to give them twenty dollars, which I did.

The loggers told us we would not get to the river on the road we had taken, so we turned around and followed them out of the woods. We drove in to Lily and I bought dinner and drinks—and a tank of gas—and Bob finally calmed down enough to speak in a normal tone of voice.

"Did you ever think maybe you should have your head examined," he said, squinting at the back bar light through ice of a Manhattan. "I'm serious. I think your brain is actually shrinking."

We fished below Slough Gundy Rapids the next morning, and as usual Bob caught three fish for my one. Later in the day we finally made it in to the Oxbow and had a spectacular evening with big browns on a high-winged fly that Bob had tied and that looked like a cross between an Adams and a Pass Lake.

Rain moved in during the night, and on the way home we stopped to fish the White River in the middle of the state. I went pretty much fishless, but Bob showed up back at the car with a nice catch of eating-sized trout.

"Tiny nymphs," he said.

A year or so after he died, Bob's wife, Judy, gave me his trout-fishing vest at a retirement party my family threw for me up at the Back-40. It was the kind of gift that rocks you back on your heels and as I held the faded old vest with its familiar stains and accouterments, I yearned for some way to turn the clock back to hear my old friend castigate me once again.

It was some weeks later in the quiet of my den that I took Bob's vest down off a hook and started to go through the pockets as an exercise in nostalgia and curiosity. There was his leader wallet, and I remembered how he always had the right leader and would complain loudly when I asked to borrow one.

The small blue bottle that he kept his dry-fly dope in was in an arm pocket, and his stream thermometer was stuffed into an inside pocket. His fly selection was modest but lethal looking, as were all of the flies that he tied. There were those Adams–Pass Lake combinations and some attractive hoppers, along with several Coachmans in size sixteen. The Coachmans were the smallest flies in the boxes.

Where were those twenty-twos he had mentioned? Maybe his eyesight in later years dictated nothing smaller than sixteens. There were also no "tiny nymphs," and I assumed that he had given those up for the same reason.

And then way down in the corner of an inside pocket, under some extra leaders and a can of fly line dressing there suddenly spilled out into my hand a very small glass vial. I held it up to the light and could not believe what I saw. Inside were a half dozen bare hooks in size six and eight, exactly the sizes you would use for worm fishing. I dug into the pocket again and there was another vial containing split-shot sinkers.

I sat for a long time staring at the vials. Could it have been? Could my old friend have been deceiving me all of those years and, when conditions called for it, had he resorted to worm fishing?

It would have been easy enough, tying on a hook and sinker and tearing apart a stump or turning over a rock to find worms.

I tried to recall specific occasions, but all of our fishing trips together seemed to blur into one long session of pleasure, despite the harangues that I suffered. I obviously deserved most of Bob's scolding, and it did serve the purpose of teaching me a few things, like the importance of checking the gas gauge before you head into the woods. I tried to remember some of those times that were so fishless for me and yet productive for Bob, but the best I could do was a detail or two about the time we stopped at the White River just after the rain. Had he "resorted" that time? Knowing that the trout were feasting on earthworms that the rain had washed into the stream, had Bob done it to me—tied on a worm hook and then given me that business later about "tiny nymphs"?

I'll never know, of course. And I really don't care. It's just that I would have liked the opportunity to confront him with the evidence. I would have pitched my voice up into some tenor octave and I would have said, "Williams, just what the hell is this all about?"

JIMMY

IT WOULD CERTAINLY be a stretch to say that Jimmy Carter was a fishing friend, but at one point while he was President we rode down the Mississippi River on the same boat. The fact that it was the Delta Queen with several hundred people aboard of course takes something away from any intimacy we might have shared. But there was one brief, memorable interlude during which I stood at the railing of the big sternwheeler with Jimmy and his wife, Rosalynn, and talked trout fishing.

I came away from the entire experience reassured that the Carters were "just folks" and convinced that the Washington press corps was then made up largely of arrogant jerks. (I'm sure that is no longer the case, is it?)

It was the summer of 1979 and the ride down the Mississippi was, I suppose, aimed at generating some positive press for the beleaguered President. In any case, when the Delta Queen left Minneapolis, the accompanying media—less than a half dozen of us—were mostly local representatives who had not bought into the no-peanut-farmer-from-Georgia-has-enough-class-to-be-President media dictum of the day. I was with the Milwaukee Journal at the time and, was surprised to find myself with such a plum assignment while most of the big league press tried to keep up with the President and the Delta Queen from a press bus. The fact that my companions and I might have been chosen for the boat ride because of our political naiveté was not important.

For several days we rode down the river, and at each lock I sprinted for the telephone and filed an account of the experience, sometimes putting myself at risk of not getting back to the boat on time and always vaguely aware of an unusual tension in the air. The presence of the President, with the cadre of Secret Service and aides hovering in the background, apparently does that to any environment, even the relaxed environs of the Delta Queen.

In addition to reporting for my newspaper, those of us on board were supposed to function as pool reporters, but when I told press secretary Jody Powell that I did not know what that entailed and if he wanted anything out of me he would have to ask for it, he said, “Don’t worry about it. There’s a wire service guy on board.”

Later, at Powell’s request, I did do a pool story on the President and his family attending church services in a makeshift chapel in the boat’s dining room. It was not what you could call a hot news item, but it apparently satisfied Powell, if not the on-shore press.

Trying to stay on top of everything was an exhausting job for a journalist unaccustomed to the high voltage media scene. Sleep was risky, even in the middle of the night, because you never knew what might happen. At one point as we cruised downriver between towns, and everyone on board was sleeping except for a Secret Service agent or two and some of the boat crew, I stood at the railing and looked out over the deep shadows of the river bottom. We were traveling through what was apparently an undeveloped area and there were no lights in sight, not even the occasional boat light or campfire.

The soft rumble of the boat’s engine was like the purring of a big cat over the expanse of deserted darkness, and I was enjoying the temporary respite from the pressures of the assignment. I’m not sure how long I stood there in the unusual solitude, but it was long enough to drift off into a daze of sorts, and then from way off in the darkness there came a single hoarse shout: “HAAAAAAAAY, JIMMMMMMIEEEEEE.”

“Jimmy” was, of course, sleeping in his stateroom, and the shouter must have known that, but it apparently didn’t matter. All during the previous evening and late on into the night, the riverbanks had been lined with crowds and campfires and shouting people. They had all long since disappeared, however, and it is possible that the shout had emanated from the coals of one of those campfire beer parties, perhaps from someone roused by a stressed bladder just as the brightly lighted Delta Queen came purring around the bend like a square-cornered spaceship.

There was only that one shout, and then the river bottom was quiet again, and I had a journalist's desire to somehow transverse the darkness and space in order to find the man who had shouted. I would liked to have asked him why he was out there in the darkness, and how long he had been there, and what he thought of "Jimmy"? Most of us have little or no contact with world leaders, and it would have been interesting to find out more about the man who must have gone to considerable trouble to put himself in position to shout a middle-of-the-night greeting to his sleeping President. It hadn't been fifteen minutes of fame, certainly, but it had been personal contact, talking to the President, sort of.

I went to bed, eventually, and woke to a strange rhythmic thump-thump-thump out on the deck, followed by another thump-thump-thump. It was the President getting in his morning jogging, and the second series of thumps had been the presidential staffer who was assigned to follow along. It isn't every day that a nondescript reporter is awakened by the footsteps of the President, and I lay there in the bunk and savored the experience briefly.

Later in the day as we rode along the southwestern edge of Wisconsin, I asked Powell if the President knew that he was traveling past some of the best trout fishing in the country.

"No," Powell said. "Why don't you come and tell him about it."

And so I found myself at the railing standing between Jimmy and Rosalynn, extolling the virtues of Wisconsin's trout streams, with particular emphasis on the big browns that you can catch on grasshopper flies in August. The President seemed interested in that, and he said that perhaps a muddler fly would work. I agreed, not choosing to point out that a muddler is usually fished wet and we were talking dry flies here.

Coincidentally, Jimmy and I had both fished Yellowstone waters the previous summer, and we talked about how we both used woolly worm flies to catch big cutthroat trout. I said they were beautiful fish, all about sixteen inches long, and Jimmy looked at me and said he caught thirteen trout and one of them was eighteen inches long.

Just for a second I considered telling him about the nineteen incher I had caught earlier in the season during the hex hatch. But I let it pass.

It happened to be the First Lady's fifty-second birthday that day and I congratulated Jimmy on his choice of a fishing vest and hat as birthday gifts for her.

"How did you know about that?" he said, with a tinge of irritation in his voice.

"I told him," Rosalynn said. And she had—earlier when I had met her at breakfast and asked what the President had given her for her birthday.

The President flashed his famous toothy grin, and said that nothing about his or Rosalynn's trout fishing could ever be as private as he would like it.

We talked some more about various flies—girdle bugs were mentioned, and various hopper ties—and then it was time for the President to get ready to greet people at the next stop.

My time on the boat ended shortly thereafter, and I got onto the press bus to find myself suddenly attacked by an irate capital press corps whose members pointed fingers and shouted that those of us on the boat had not done our duty under the rules of pool reporting. It was an unpleasant experience, like suddenly finding yourself in the midst of a pack of unruly, yapping dogs. The attack went to our character and professionalism, and subsided only when some of those who had been with me on the boat agreed that we would all sit down in the press tent and carefully reconstruct everything that had transpired during our boat ride.

Once we arrived at the press tent, the attack resumed, however, and I was suddenly moved to rip paper from typewriter, gather up my notebooks, and give a brief farewell speech that suggested an impossible and obscene exercise for the hotshot capital press corps. Whereupon I exited the press tent and headed for the nearest tavern for a cold beer.

Several weeks after the event, I received a very nice photograph from the White House in which I appear to be using a pen to give fly casting instructions to an attentive President and First Lady. They had both graciously autographed the photo "To a fellow fisherman," and I have since kept it hanging where I can use it as a reminder of a number of things.

First, there is the President, who is the epitome of those whose ambitions put them in positions where their trout fishing becomes either offensively artificial or of such low priority that it just never gets done.

Then there is Rosalynn, who perhaps recognized many of the impediments that will forever plague her famous fishing husband, and she therefore develops enough of an interest in trout fishing to provide some untainted angling companionship.

To the left in the photo there is a smiling Jody Powell, who is obviously trying to give his boss a little trout-talk diversion and who certainly knows the contrary ways of the Washington press corps better than any naive midwest journalist ever could.

The photo, of course, also reminds me of the press corps as it was represented that day. From my unpleasant experience with it, and from many things that have happened since, questions are posed about my profession, about its avowed objectivity, its inclination to a pack mentality, its appetite for the negative to the point where being nice is perceived as being weak, and its apparent conviction that no wound is so old or obscure that it can't be reopened to make a headline.

Then the photo reminds me of the man who shouted out of the darkness that night on the Mississippi. I identify with him. We are all of us more or less shouting out of the darkness, even the President, who says he would like his trout fishing to be more private.

"HAAAAAAAAY, JIMMMMMMIEEEEEE!"

IN A PIG'S EAR

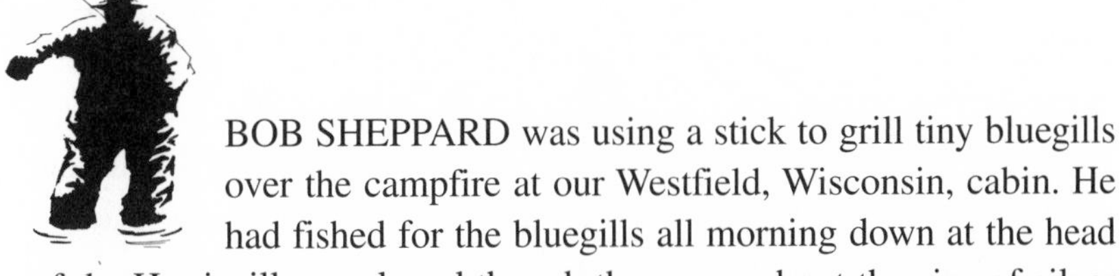

BOB SHEPPARD was using a stick to grill tiny bluegills over the campfire at our Westfield, Wisconsin, cabin. He had fished for the bluegills all morning down at the head of the Harrisville pond, and though they were about the size of silver dollars, they were fresh caught and Bob loved fresh fish. When he had what he considered the perfect blackened bluegill, he would chew on it, bones and all, to the entertainment of several of my sons who had been conditioned to shun fish bones, even small ones, as more or less deadly. Bob was surprised when they expressed their amazement.

"They won't hurt you," he said of the bluegill bones. "In fact they help clean out your insides."

My own culinary experiences with Bob went back to the army field rations that we sometimes shared and that he would spice up with his own cache of hot seasoning to a point that made you yearn for mess tent blandness.

Bob Sheppard and I met in 1951 when he arrived as a replacement in our infantry platoon, and we buttoned a couple of those old army "shelter halves" together to ward off a cold, wet Korean snowstorm.

As army buddies, we were something of an odd couple: big-city kid/farm boy, draftee/volunteer, black/white.

"You enlisted!" Bob said in an expression of abject incredulity when he discovered that my serial number began with RA, which was an enlistee's identity. And through the long years of our friendship, he would toss that "you enlisted!" phrase out at what he thought were appropriate times, most often when I found myself beset by life's woes.

Following our year of shooting-war unpleasantness in Korea, there was a long lapse in our association as Bob returned to Chicago and I went back to Wisconsin. Years passed—almost twenty of them—and then one night Bob showed up at the cabin, and we picked up where we had left off, me extolling the virtues of Wisconsin life while Bob expanded on his view of our country ways as being just a cut above barbaric.

I was anxious to introduce Bob to the joys of trout fishing, and he consented to follow me along the stream one evening. I had lent him some fly fishing gear but he obviously had no feel for it, and when it got dark and the mosquitoes began gnawing at him as he stumbled about in the swamp, he said, "Stokes, you have enlisted in dumbness again, but I haven't and I am getting the hell out of here."

Trout fishing, he later announced, was a sport for the demented. "Fishing is supposed to be relaxing," he said. "How can you relax when you are up to your fanny in muck, and bugs are sucking out all your blood?"

Bob was a skilled survivor in the big city, constantly watching over his shoulder for threats from his fellow men, and aware of the need to secure everything and everyone with double locks, if not weaponry. He found it highly amusing that once when my car was in a Chicago restaurant parking lot someone broke open the trunk and stole a new pair of hunting boots.

"You don't keep that kind of thing in your trunk," Bob said, "particularly if you have out-of-state license plates."

Bob's survivor skills, however, did not transfer to the woods, and he was not at ease with such harmless creatures as owls, rodents, and the occasional fox or coyote. And he did not appreciate my talent for calling up barred owls, hinting that there was something perverse about a man and an owl arguing with each other.

Most of the time, Bob lived alone on the South Side of Chicago. Other times he shared his small, neat house with a guard dog of some breed, usually either a German shepherd or a gangly Rottweiler. When we first renewed our acquaintance and Bob began to visit us at the cabin, he had a nice old German shepherd named Beau, who seemed as out of place in the woods as Bob often did. Bob would tie Beau to a tree and the dog would lie there peacefully and watch the surrounding activity with what seemed to be a puzzled canine expression.

"He's a city dog," Bob would say if anyone commented on Beau's quizzical demeanor.

If the rest of us accepted Beau on his terms, my springer spaniel, Doc, did not. It was his territory, Doc believed, and what right did this big damn police dog have to be on it? No matter the lectures and the threats, Doc would not stay away from Beau, but would instead sneak in to pick a fight the minute I took my eyes off him. Beau fought reluctantly and only in defense, and given his size he always won, frequently ending up by using his superior weight to more or less hold Doc down on his back while Doc snarled and snapped viciously.

This all came to a sad end one day with an incident in Bob's South Chicago home. A young man in Bob's community made the mistake of breaking into Bob's house when Bob was not home but Beau was. Beau chased the young man upstairs and into Bob's bedroom where the burglar slammed the door shut and abruptly found himself imprisoned by a dog. It was not a pleasant situation to be in, obviously, and the young man did what a lot of young men do when they get into trouble: using Bob's bedroom telephone, he called his mother.

Mom then called the police to report that a dog had chased her son into a house and had him trapped in an upstairs room.

The Chicago police responded, with drawn guns apparently, and when Beau continued to do his job by guarding Bob's house against all intruders, even those in uniforms, the cops shot Beau dead in Bob's living room.

The young burglar was rescued and sent home to Mama, and the cops left, leaving Beau's bloody body on Bob's living room floor which is where Bob found it.

The incident did not make the evening news—not gory enough apparently—but it did show up later in a piece by syndicated columnist Mike Royko.

And that was all that happened. The would-be house thief was never charged with anything, and Bob never learned why the police shot his "police" dog.

"What are you gonna do?" Bob said, philosophic about the cruel ways of the big city.

During my tenure with the *Chicago Tribune*, Bob often invited me out to his house for dinner, and it was always a treat. He was a very good cook, and I especially liked the fish dinners that he served. Bob would also sometimes prepare what he called a "soul food" dish that was new to me, and he took great delight in surprising me with these homey concoctions, often withholding information about their contents until I had eaten them. One night when I sat down to his dining room table for pork and sauerkraut, I was startled to see a plate on which there were several pig ears. They were, of course, cooked and garnished, but they were unmistakably pig ears, and they were intended to complement the main course of the meal.

I have consumed my share of pickled pigs feet and hocks, and tried chitlins, but I had never eaten a pig ear. Bob knew that, of course, and I knew that he was watching out of the corner of his eye for my reaction to his unique side dish.

We sat down to dinner and when Bob passed me the pig ears I made no comment but helped myself to one as if I ate them every day. And I ate that ear, every last gristly bit of it, trying to overcome the lack of conditioning for such unusual fare by telling myself I was eating the tongue of an old shoe.

Bob didn't say a word about the pig ears as we ate, and when we were finished with the meal, which was delicious in all other respects, I complimented him on his culinary skills. And then over a final glass of wine I said, "Thanks for the dinner, Sheppard, but damn you, don't ever serve me another pig ear."

Bob almost fell off his chair in spasms of knee-slapping laughter.

And he almost fell off his chair the last time he came to the cabin, but on that occasion it was because he dozed off after a session at our table during which he consumed prodigious amounts of my wife Betty's spaghetti and meat balls. As he caught himself in his slouch toward a snooze, and his eyes flew open, he scowled over at my laughter and said, "Why don't you take your little fish stick down by the creek and stand in the muck with the mosquitoes so I can have a little nap?"

Which is what I did, thinking as I did so how Bob's friendship over the years had enriched a clan of racially isolated innocents in more ways than I can imagine. He was not black, and we were not white. Bob somehow made it that way, and since his heart gave out some time ago, I'll never get to ask him just how he managed it.

DAD

EXCEPT FOR A LITTLE brook trout fishing on Engle Creek when he was growing up, my father did not really get into fishing until he retired at the age of sixty-five. It was as if the provisions of the Social Security Act and his pension plan contained a clause that said, "Okay, Forrest P. Stokes, you have worked your butt off for lo these many years and you may now go fishing."

Dad was a member of that rapidly disappearing generation that was conditioned by the Great Depression of the 1930s to work-work-work. But Dad never complained about it. He simply did not go fishing or do much of anything else that took him away from his dual role of farmer and crane operator for the county highway department. To Dad and many of his contemporaries, the only thing better than one job was two jobs, and the real joys of life were as basic as a well-fed family and clothes to protect against the cruelties of winter.

But then with his children grown and an adequate retirement income guaranteed for him and my mother, Dad and a few of his friends decided that they could actually go fishing. That they would pattern their fishing in such a way that it involved a lot of work and had aspects of the old tribal chiefs going out to lay in seasonal provisions was not at all surprising. Without this kind of discipline prevailing, they could not possibly have enjoyed themselves.

In the summer, their fishing trips frequently took them to the Ignace, Ontario, area where they fished for walleye and northern pike.

In the winter, they would set tip-ups on the ice of Long Lake near their homes in northwest Wisconsin and catch more northerns and walleyes.

But for these veterans of the big economic war, it was not all as simple as it sounds. Their primary consideration was to do their fishing at the lowest possible cost, and if there had been a way for them to make their own fish hooks they would have done so in a minute. As it was, they caught their own minnows for winter fishing and stored their own night crawlers for panfish occasions.

The minnows were caught by hook and line in the fall when Dad and his most frequent fishing partner, Pete Manor, would hike in to one of the small area streams and load buckets and cans with shiners and dace. The minnows were then stored in a big screen cage along the Red Cedar River in Rice Lake. There, on frosty winter mornings with the river vaporizing like spilled tea, Dad and his cronies would stop and fill their minnow buckets and invariably talk about the current price of minnows at the local bait outlet. Having thus reassured themselves that they were "saving" money, they could then more comfortably head out to spend the day on the ice.

On the all too few times that I was able to join them, the routine varied only slightly. There would be the telephone call the preceding night, and then my mother would get up early and pack the lunch material, which usually included sandwiches and thermoses of hot coffee. And most of the time there would also be a generous package of raw hamburger, along with big onions and buttered buns for the traditional noon cookout.

The road twisted up along the west shore of the lake and then at one point there was a turnoff that led down onto the ice. Yesterday's vehicle tracks were sometimes clogged by snow that had drifted in during the night, but Dad and his friends drove lumbering old, big-wheeled pickups that were undaunted by this kind of impediment.

They would head out across the ice in the direction of Greenhagen's bay and there they would stop to set up for the day. The tip-ups would go out first, into holes that they made by the ringing thud of ice chisels in the days before hand and motorized augers.

Once the baited lines were set, three holes were made in the ice for the windbreak, which consisted of wooden poles and a piece of heavy canvas. The stove, handmade in Pete Manor's shop, was then assembled, the stove pipe inserted, and the fire was built.

No matter the severity of the weather, this arrangement of windbreak and stove immediately put the elements at bay. There could not have been a more comfortable place to be on a ringing cold Wisconsin winter day than between the stove and the sheltering canvas, while you watched out over the scattered tip-ups.

Sometimes the ice would crack and rumble as if one of last summer's thunderstorms was breaking out of a deep-water grave, and other days the gray of winter would become as thick as soup, and snow would begin to fall as if the sky had ruptured.

At midday when the frying pan clattered down onto the stove and the onions and hamburger began to sizzle, the tantalizing aroma was enough to make a snowman salivate. If it were possible to duplicate even a portion of those conditions for commercial purposes, the reigning fast food joints would fold like circus tents before the competition.

I don't think Dad and Pete and their friends were ever skunked, though some days they had to be satisfied with a modest catch of "hammer handle" northerns. Usually, however, there would be larger fish, and the excitement of their fishing was due in large measure to never knowing just what kind of a critter was down there mouthing the minnow and getting ready to run off into the green weeds.

The "hot" moments of the day for the fishermen occurred when two or three of them huddled over a hole in the ice and kept a careful bare-handed control on a line that had been yanked just hard enough to send the tip-up's flag up to wave in the breeze. Muttered opinions and advice would be offered as the quiet wait went on, and then if there was another run, the hook would be set and the battle joined. The hand-over-hand retrieve would then begin, and anyone who has done such battle knows that there is a strange, primitive thrill in being connected to a fish without the interceding assistance of a fishing rod. Under no other circumstances does the head shaking and writhing of a big northern pike communicate itself more directly to a fisherman's soul or heart or whatever it is that registers such stimuli.

I did not have the good fortune to be along when Dad or Pete or any of the others caught a really big fish, but I heard about them. They would tell how the fish made long runs and how they missed it with the gaff and how it wouldn't fit through the fishing hole. Whenever they finished a fish story like that there would be quiet out there on the ice around the stove, and everyone would think about big fish and glance out at the tip-ups.

Dad and his friends stuffed the hammer-handle northerns back into the ice holes, but they brought home everything else they caught. They were, after all, the chiefs out on an expedition for provisions, and while they might have been enjoying themselves, they needed a burlap sack weighted down with frozen pike to give them a sense of satisfaction. And the day did not end until the fish had all been sliced into fillets, wrapped in freezer paper, and stowed away.

They were the same way with summer fishing. A Canada northern or walleye won its freedom usually only after a larger one had been caught to take its place on the limited-out stringer.

It was a ten-hour drive from where Dad and Pete lived to the Ignace area where they fished, and they would make the trip almost nonstop, rattling up along Lake Superior's north shore to Thunder Bay and then making that long run west across the bedrock and muskeg to Ignace. They traveled in Pete's old pickup, a vehicle with four-wheel drive capacity that Pete had rescued from the salvage yard and which always impressed them with its thirst for fuel. They pulled a trailer that Frog Hollis, another of their fishing cronies, had adapted to haul two boats and motors and all of the rest of their gear.

In Ignace they rented an economy cabin and from this they went out each day to fish the various area lakes, many of which were a real challenge to get to because of impossible roads or launching sites. This meant that each morning they got out of bed, cooked breakfast, and made a lunch and then loaded everything up and drove to the lake of the day, where there was either a muddy, rocky, back-breaking launch site or a road that was navigable only part of the time and frequently left them either stuck in the mud or hung up on a boulder.

Then at the end of a full day of fishing, the entire process would have to be reversed—and the launch sites were always uphill on the way out. Then when they arrived back in Ignace they had to not only unload all the gear and sort everything out but also clean and package the fish of the day, often a huge stringer of northerns or walleye. Then and only then could they think about cooking their evening meal. Evening, hell! The first time I went with them, it was ten o'clock at night before anyone thought about eating.

The camp where they stayed had a freezer and each day—before eating supper, of course—someone would take the day's catch, all neatly wrapped and labeled, and put it in the freezer. The freezer contents were like the running score of a marathon, and close tabs were kept on how many of each fish species were there.

The first trip I made with Dad and Pete required a certain period of indoctrination, and it was three or four days before my aching muscles and frazzled brain forced me to conclude that while I might be on a "fun" fishing trip, it was, by god, going to be a lot of work.

One place in particular that they liked to fish was, by any normal standards, a fly-in lake. Not so for Dad and Pete and their ilk. They left camp in the early morning, and with their old wooden trailer loaded with the boats behind their rattling pickup they drove a circular route over rocky, gravel roads that seemed destined to lead to Alaska. At the end of the gravel there was a trail that might give pause to a moose, but they bounced over it like indifferent tourists. Then there was a hill so steep and so washed out that it was literally unnavigable. They navigated it, with rocks flying and tires screeching around the boulders. The hill was followed by another stretch of trail that wound through a swamp where you could sink an army tank, but which they breezed through as if they knew what they were doing.

The first time I went in to this lake with them, I was sure that all of them had lost their reason. A full day of some of the best northern pike fishing I have ever experienced did little to convince me otherwise because I kept thinking, Lord save us, we've got to traverse the whole damn thing in reverse in order to get back to camp.

The fact is, they did once get stranded at this lake when a sudden downpour absolutely destroyed portions of the trail. They spent the night in a trapper's shack, and as near as I could interpret their accounts of it, it was a great experience except that they had to stand outside in the rain and clean a bunch of big northerns.

Another trip that I made with them marked the last fishing excursion that Frog was able to make. He had been stricken by one of those horrendous afflictions that slowly rusts the brain, and it had reduced Frog from a take-charge guy to a bumbling sort who had to be led to the bathroom. Pete and Frog had fished together since high school, and Pete was determined to give Frog one more shot at it. It was one of those pure acts of charity and friendship that go unrecognized, and I will always remember how Pete spent the entire week patiently explaining to Frog how to fasten a bait onto his leader and how to carry his tackle box from the pickup to the boat.

And, of course, another thing I will remember about those Canada trips with the "tribal elders" is how Dad and I fished together, just the two of us in the boat hour after hour, and how we talked about so many things.

"We should have gone fishing more when you were a kid," Dad said at one point.

"Yeah," I said, "but that's what I get for being a Depression baby."

LAUGHING WHILE WET

AMONG THE MOLDY axioms that surface when outdoor types gather is one which holds that life deals you one special marital partner and one special hunting dog. To that must be added one special fishing companion. I have been blessed beyond measure in all three categories. But this is about fishing, and the many hours that I spent trout fishing with John Lawton are like the diamonds in a rhinestone life. They catch the light of memory like nothing else, and if they hadn't been so damn much fun I would be reduced to the maudlin.

The first time I saw John he was fighting a losing battle with Little Slough Gundy Rapids on the Wolf River. He had taken one step too many in an effort to reach a particular slick, and the river had said, "No, I don't think so," and then it had more or less grabbed John's waders and was slowly easing him toward an inglorious dunking.

Above the roar of the rapids you could hear John's whoops and curses . . . and laughter.

Ah yes, that laughter. I came to know it over the years as one of John's outstanding attributes. No matter what outrageous or even serious—at least by our warped judgment—thing we were involved in, if the laughter wasn't already flavoring the scene it was just waiting to erupt.

So on this occasion, just as he was swept off his feet and carried downstream with only his head and arms above water, he was laughing loud enough to startle porcupines.

The river washed him through the pool below the rapids as he struggled to stay upright and keep his rod from being smashed. It was quite

a performance, like a sodden and stumbling Gene Kelly singing in the rapids instead of the rain. Finally John was able to regain his footing and slosh through the boulders to the riverbank, water splashing out over the tops of his waders and dripping off his eyebrows. He grinned and said, "I wanted to go through that pool to wake up the trout."

John was a labor lawyer and spent a lot of time around the state capitol in Madison. He was instrumental in drafting much of Wisconsin's prevailing municipal labor law, and in later years he served for a long time on the Department of Natural Resources board where his trout fishing experience served him and the state well.

But on this day he looked like the proverbial drowned rat.

"Damn river," he said as we walked back toward the shack. "It either knocks you on your ass or pushes you out of the best fishing water."

Back at the shack, John got out of his waders amid cascades of tannin-colored water, and then sat in his wet clothes next to the stove and sipped brandy.

"Getting dunked always gives you a thirst," he said.

I had been invited along on the fishing trip by Art Jensen, who ran an auto repair business in Madison and considered John one of his best customers. "It's a real challenge to keep him on the road," Jensen once told me. "He has no more mechanical sense than a squirrel."

Jensen added that his mechanics all liked to work on John's car since its undercarriage was always clean and free of oil and grease because of John's propensity for driving brushy, grass-covered back roads or across fields and sometimes even swamps.

There are images of that first Wolf River trip that remain exquisitely clear to this day—John's dunking and the trout that leaped for a fly the next day just as I yanked it away. I was more or less new to fly fishing, particularly on a big river, and while John and the others were free with advice they didn't waste a lot of their fishing time acting as guides. Once John helped me cross a rapids because I did not have felt-bottom wading sandals and without them it was almost impossible to stand up in the river. We struggled across the rolling boulders, me clutching his arm and him laughing, and then, once across the river, he disappeared upstream and left me with the advice to "try an Adams."

I didn't even know what an Adams looked like, but it didn't matter because it was late afternoon and a hatch of some kind emerged and the fish began to feed all over the river. I was flailing away at a feeding fish just below one of the car-sized boulders, and that was when I jerked the fly away from a big brown. The trout's leap startled me and it forever set the hook in my psyche on the beauty and mystery of the Wolf River.

My willingness to serve as the chef on that first fishing trip pretty much set in stone the arrangement between John and me for the next twenty-five years. It was not that I had any particular culinary skills. Far from it. As my family will attest, the response to my making a move in the direction of the kitchen has always been a suggestion to call Pizza Hut. But John hated to cook, for himself or anyone else, and it was probably just as well because his wife, Esther, said he was a disaster at any kind of food preparation, even down to making sandwiches. His specialty, she said, was "hash blacks."

No matter what I threw together in the big iron skillets at the Wolf or at John's haunted house near Westfield or at my cabin, John would eat heaping plates of it, smack his lips, and say, "Damn, Stokes, that was delicious. Where'd you learn to cook like that?"

Then he would head for the nearest cot and collapse into a snoring heap.

It is unfortunate but true that my camp cooking depended for its palatability on the liberal use of bacon grease or some other equally lethal artery clogger. Also I got pretty good at boiling potatoes. Through all of our years together, I never prepared anything that John didn't gobble up and then rave about. And this despite the fact that at the end of a two- or three-day excursion, our digestive systems were likely to be so out of whack that there was genuine risk involved in ignoring the slightest sphincter muscle signal. When this circumstance overcame him with particular vengeance, John would say, "Must have a touch of the flu." Once when he was thus stricken, John was driving back from the Wolf when he made an emergency stop in a farmer's field that just happened to be under the surveillance of a game warden who was watching for late-summer deer shiners.

Unbeknowst to John, the warden watched him through binoculars and was apparently so mystified by what he saw that he followed John down the road and pulled him over to inquire just what John had been up to back there.

In telling the story later, John said, "I looked him in the eye and said, 'I crapped in my pants,' and the warden stared at me for a couple of minutes and then just backed away from the car without saying a word."

John's Wolf River cabin is a one-room affair that was built of cedar and pine by a couple of local carpenters. During the course of the construction, one of the carpenters—a tough old "Kaintuck"—accidentally sawed into his hand to the extent that by anyone else's standard he needed medical attention. But he wrapped a soiled handkerchief around his wound and kept on carpentering. As a result, most of the roof boards show the carpenter's bloody hand prints to this day, and when you lie on one of the cots you can see them and speculate about what the scene must have been like.

"We tried to get him to go to the doctor," John said, "but he just drank more brandy and stayed on the job, blood all over the goddamn place."

The carpenters also had enough cedar left over to put up a one-holer, which caused several instances of exaggerated consternation down through the years when it became necessary to either repair or move the structure.

The door never did work, and finally the entire front fell off, which gave an occupant a sweeping view of the cabin and its environs. This open architecture, John claimed, gave his outhouse a Frank Lloyd Wright appearance.

In addition to my signing on as cook, another thing about that first Wolf River weekend that set the stage for our subsequent rendezvous was the rain that seemed to be forever sneaking in during the night and turning the quarter-mile long, rock-strewn, rutted driveway into a grease pit.

On that initial trip, the rain filtered down through the trees and fell onto the cabin roof in the darkness to sound like the patter of a thousand tiny feet. The next morning, while I was working up a breakfast of fried potatoes, eggs and bacon . . . and grease, John said, "We're stuck in here so we might as well go fishing."

I didn't know at the time what he meant, but I soon learned. Once the mixture of black soil and leaves in the tire tracks of the driveway got wet, it became as slippery as our breakfast bacon grease. The rain had slowed to a fine mist on this particular morning, and it was apparently John's theory that the driveway would dry out some under this reduced rate of precipitation and we would then be able to drive out to the road. I learned later that John's theories were unfailingly structured around the opportunity to go trout fishing. He knew that the driveway was not going to dry out, and he knew that there was going to be hell to pay in getting our vehicles out to solid traction, but he also knew from experience that misty, gray days could produce some fantastic Wolf River fishing.

He did catch some trout that morning, and I have a vivid image of those too, glistening on the ice of his cooler as he slipped them out of his creel and said that he had promised his family a trout dinner.

It was then, only after the trout issue had been taken care of, that attention was turned to extracting ourselves from the woods.

Without ceremony, John jumped into his old station wagon and began to fishtail up the road in a cloud of flying mud. Jensen groaned and watched as John somehow got his vehicle crossways in the road with both sets of wheels hanging out over the boulders.

That meant that someone had to walk into Lily to summon Claude, the local mechanic who had an old dilapidated wrecker. The shortest route—three miles or so—was down the railroad track, and I volunteered to make the trip, which seemed to be fine with the rest of them, especially John, who was reaching for his fly rod before I had turned around.

When I got to town and explained the situation to Claude, he turned and shouted to his wife, "Watch the gas pumps, I gotta go get John Lawton again."

As we rode out of town, Claude said that whenever he saw John show up in Lily he knew it would just be a matter of time until John needed to be pulled out of some kind of trouble.

Claude slipped and slid down the driveway and then, in the process of jerking on John's vehicle, Claude's wrecker somehow straddled a rock and a big stream of black oil poured out to make the mud even more slippery.

By the time everything was back out on the road, everyone was covered with mud, there were several new dents in John's station wagon, several of us had wrenched backs, and Claude's wrecker had lost all of its oil and was making a strange noise.

It was, I was to learn, an all too frequent kind of thing. But when the passion was on and there were trout to be caught, the driveway that sloped down toward the shack seemed like a super highway as we arrived at the start of a fishing trip. Invariably we would forget about previous difficulty and fish until the rain came and we were stranded again.

At some point we began making brief pencil notes on the inside walls of the cabin to record what, on the surface, seems to be an endless stream of disasters. Along with dates there are such notations as "Rained all night. River at flood. No fish. Snow. Only two small browns. Flat tire."

But when I get back to the Wolf now to review those notes, there is such a flood of golden memories that I realize the little disaster notations on the wall are only like bookmarks in great tomes. And then I hear the echoes of John's laughter.

JUST OVER THE HILL

ALL TROUT FISHERMEN get lost, but John Lawton elevated it to an art form. There is no way to know how many extra miles we walked through the years, stumbling about in the darkness like demented bears just because John thought he knew where the car or the bridge or the trail was. "It's just over the hill," I can hear him saying from somewhere ahead as we struggled through the woods in the blackness of night, rods and nets tangling in the brush, boulders barking our shins, sticks poking at our eyes, and mosquitoes swarming by the thousand. And all of this, of course, as the flashlights slowly lost their power and finally went completely dead.

When two people get lost, it is only fair to divide up the blame, but John always seemed so sure that his course was better than any I might suggest that I unfailingly deferred to him. Maybe his lawyer inclination to be assertive had something to do with his resistance to my opinion, but I think the reality is that John somehow believed that through the power of his intellect he could influence his inner compass and the alignment of the Earth's detritus to bring us out to the right spot. Something like that, anyway.

It was only years later that I began to carry a compass, which John always disputed, saying, "Stokes, goddamnit, I don't care what that thing says, the car is not over there."

As a result I also began to carry extra flashlight batteries because I knew that even with a compass we were going to get lost.

And it wasn't just at night that we got lost. On a gray, sunless day on the Wolf River we once spent most of the afternoon trying to fight our way back out to the road. In all fairness, this had not been all John's fault, but I blame him for not recognizing the contrary circumstance that kept us in the woods for hours.

It was a good fishing day, and browns were feeding with certain delicacy on what John called "that big high-winged fly." Three of us had walked in to separate sections of the river and after several hours of fishing I ran into John and we started walking out to the car. There were no trails, and once into the woods and away from the river it was impossible to maintain a constant course.

After a time, I suggested to John that we were going in a circle, having noted what seemed to be a rotted old birch that I was sure we had passed a half hour ago.

We paused, and just then way off in the distance we heard the honking of a car horn.

"That's Howie's car," John said. "Let's go."

We headed off in the direction of the car horn and walked for twenty minutes or so, and we obviously veered off course because next time we heard the horn it was coming from way off to our left.

"Damn," John said. "It's hard to go straight in this jungle."

We walked some more and when we stopped again, the sound of the horn seemed to be coming from an entirely different direction.

John and I looked at each other, wiping off sweat and mosquitoes, and with some resignation, changed our direction and headed for the sound we had heard.

This kind of thing went on for a very long time, the sound of the car horn jerking us about in the woods as if we were flies on the end of a whip.

"Godalmighty," John said at one point, "we must have walked ten miles."

Finally we stumbled out onto the road where we were sure we had just heard the car horn, but the car was not there.

We collapsed beside the road, and when he had caught his breath, John said, "You know what that dumb bastard has been doing?"

I shook my head.

"Instead of staying in one place and honking the horn, Howie has been running up and down the road honking from all over hell."

Just then Howie came roaring down the road and stopped beside us. "Jeezz," he said, "I thought you guys were lost. I've been driving around honking the horn. Didn't you hear it?"

John looked at him and shook his head. "Where's the brandy?" he said.

Howie Kaline later gave up trout fishing and moved to California, but not before getting into trouble again with his car horn. On this occasion, another of our fishing cronies—Hilding Haag, a tall, distinguished-looking Swede with a twitching mustache—was answering a call of nature beside a grassy clearing way back in the woods. It was a windy day with lots of leaf noise, and just as Hilding settled in to his task, Howie came driving over a little rise in the trail and saw Hilding whose back—and backside—were turned in Howie's direction. Howie turned off the engine and let his car coast silently until it was just a few feet from Hilding and then he blasted on the car horn.

Hilding, who had not been aware of Howie's presence until that second, later claimed that not only had Howie's "inexcusable meanness" placed him at risk for a heart attack, but it also sent his bowels into such shock that he was severely constipated for weeks.

John went into paroxysms of laughter when he heard the story, and once he got rested up from our session of following the roaming car horn through the woods, he laughed about that too.

One warm June night after a productive session of fishing the hex hatch on the Mecan River, John said there was a shortcut to the road through the "little" tamarack swamp off to the left.

The word "shortcut" should be considered an alarm bell when used by anyone who is not sitting at home in an easy chair. It should have been particularly alarming when used by John, rather like hearing Willie Sutton say, "Let's stop at the bank."

But the swamp couldn't be that big, I reasoned, and so we headed through it. The mosquitoes were especially bad this night, not easing up with the shank of darkness as they often did but seeming to increase in numbers and aggressiveness as the night wore on. As the swamp swallowed us up, it was as if we had invaded the mosquitoes' very home and tens of thousands of them were rallying to drive us off.

Tamarack, as most trout fishermen know, is one of the worst plants on God's green earth for reaching out to snag a fly rod or line, and so our progress through the swamp was frequently stopped as we struggled to untangle one rod or another. Thus presented with a stationary target, the mosquitoes called in even more reserves and there was a blood letting the likes of which has rarely been experienced.

I could hear John muttering and cursing as he threshed about ahead of me, and it began to dawn on me that we were in what was quickly becoming an intolerable situation.

John apparently came to the same conclusion, and after an exceptionally loud string of blasphemy, the crashing ahead of me intensified as John began to try to run through the swamp, heedless of his tangled rod and net. The result was a mighty crashing and cursing, and while I knew it to be a foolhardy thing to do, I followed suit.

We ran like crazed bulls, or rather, tried to run, jerking our rods and nets free and falling on our faces in the nettles and muck, and rising only to fall again.

The mosquitoes apparently thought it was some kind of game because they joined in enthusiastically, and it seemed to be a tossup as to whether we would die of exhaustion and frustration or whether the mosquitoes would suck us completely dry of blood.

We finally fell out of the swamp and staggered to the car where we collapsed in a kind of embalmed misery. Our waders were ripped, most of the eyes had been stripped off our rods, our nets were torn, and we were bleeding from scratches and hundreds of mosquito bites.

"Fun, huh?" John gasped as he tried to scratch himself in ten different places.

On another night—this time on the Wolf River—I thought for a time that we might be permanently lost. John's teenage son Jack was along, and we had driven in as far as we could to the river's famous Oxbow from the east side of the river. These roads have since been closed and the easier access is from the west, but on this night we drove John's old station wagon to a fork in the logging roads and walked on down to start fishing at Cedar Rapids.

As usual on the Wolf, it was an interesting evening. There were several hatches and between catching fish and struggling to stay upright as the river roared along between the boulders, we had been royally entertained. Also as usual, John had taken the biggest and most trout, and had paid the price of being dunked several times. I had also taken on some water when I lost my footing as I tried to put a fly on the deep side of a boulder. But it was a warm night and being wet was not all that much of a problem.

We fished until eleven o'clock or so, and then we started up the hill in the direction of the car, John as usual leading the way, Jack following and me bringing up the rear. And then I do not know how he did it because the trail was not that far away, but John got us lost. Suddenly we were on one of those very steep, boulder-strewn hillsides where the next step could mean a thirty-foot plunge down onto a rock pile.

"I think the car's just over the hill," John said, using his familiar line, but this time without the usual ring of conviction in his voice.

We went "over the hill," and then over the next hill, or maybe the same hill from another direction, and there was no sign of the car or even of a trail.

We had used up a lot of flashlight battery during the course of our fishing, and our lights were beginning to fade. John's in particular was producing less light than a firefly.

"Give me your flashlight, Stokes," John said. "I think I know where we are."

He knew where we were, all right. We were lost in the woods, and it was a big woods. Since I too had no idea where we were, I gave my flashlight to John, thinking, I guess, that since he was supposed to know the country much better than I, he would eventually get us out of it. We floundered on, moving very slowly to avoid falling into one of the rocky gorges or smashing our noses into one of the huge boulders.

When we stopped once to rest, I suggested that once it got daylight it might be easier for us to find the car. Jack giggled, and John said, "We gotta be close to it."

"Just over the hill, maybe," I said.

And then in the stillness of that pitch black night, we heard the distant roar of the rapids. We listened to it in silence for a time, and then John said, "That's what we have to do. We've got to go back to the river and start over."

And, groping our way in a Braille-like fashion because the flashlights were now all useless, that is what we did. We crawled and crept around rocks and over windfalls and sometimes toppled into sharp depressions, and then finally we were at the river's edge with the roar of the rapids filling the night like something alive and hungry.

Miraculously, the trail was right there beside the river and we followed it back to the car.

"Don't understand it," John said.

I didn't either. The only explanation, of course, is that John had led us across instead of along the trail when we first left the river. But just how he could do that, and how I could fail to notice it at the time, is a great mystery.

The night had worn us out so much that we went back to the shack and fell into our sleeping bags without supper. I had one of those strange, slightly erotic dreams in which a gorgeous woman whispered in my ear, "Just over the hill. Just over the hill."

FISH CARS

HALF THE POPULATION is driving "fish cars" these days—"sport utility vehicles" that the manufacturers say are ideal for climbing mountains and fording deep rivers. Fortunately most of these expensive gas guzzlers only go back and forth to the mall, because if they all went fishing there wouldn't be room along the rivers and lakes to park a unicycle. But there was a day when fish cars were something else, and when they really went fishing. Usually these vehicles were cast-off jalopies that rattled and smoked and stank, and had more character than Barney Fife's squad car. The late John Voelker had such a fish car—a '28 Model A Ford that he called Buckshot and could not bring himself to trade in on a jeep because of all that he and Buckshot had been through.

During the years that I fished with him, John Lawton had a number of fish cars but, unlike Voelker, John never felt any emotion for any of them. Unless, of course, you count the way he felt about the old slant-back Chevrolet after he got trapped inside of it with the bumblebees.

John was what our mechanic friend Art Jensen called a "car killer." By necessity, John kept Art more or less on retainer, and when Art came along on a fishing trip it was understood that he would bring his tools.

Most of John's fishing-car history was written along the Wolf River between the communities of Lily and Langlade because it was here that for many years John kept a special vehicle just for getting in and out of such places as the Oxbow. The "special" vehicle concept came into being at Art's suggestion after John ripped the oil pan off a new car and

then ruined the engine when he drove it all the way back to Lily to get the oil checked.

One of those early fishing cars was an old Buick station wagon that John got as a "gift" from Carl Lee, another fishing crony. It had been a "woodie" but most of the wood had rotted and fallen off, and so the roof just in back of the driver's seat had been bent over and crunched down because there was not much to hold it up and it tended to more or less flap in the breeze.

This meant that there was no visibility to the rear, and this made it difficult to maneuver in the tight confines of logging roads and mud holes. During one fishing weekend, Art took an ax to the problem and chopped a rear window in the remodeled roof. John considered this a stroke of genius and told Art he wouldn't take ten thousand dollars for his fishing wagon.

The next weekend, John bounded over a rock in his haste to get into Cedar Rapids, and the entire bottom of the engine and transmission of the old Buick was mangled beyond repair.

Claude, who ran the garage in Lily, retrieved the "dead" car at what he said was considerable trouble, and Bill Stennis sold it to a junk dealer for a lot less than it cost to tow it out of the woods.

Stennis, who with his wife, Nel, ran the corner tavern in Lily, was John's "car agent," providing parking and general oversight and brokering replacement deals when the occasion arose. With the demise of the Buick, Bill found an old Chevrolet sedan that had the kind of awkward sweeping lines that made it look like a cross between a rocket and a tractor. It was a faded black color, most of the interior handles had been broken off the doors, and one side of the windshield was cracked. When John first saw it, he exclaimed that it was obviously the classiest fishing car in the state, and that, "By god, Stokes, it's too good for you to drive."

Under normal circumstances, John not only allowed me to drive his vehicles but virtually insisted that I do so, which freed him up to relax and criticize the way I did things.

It was our custom to drive to Lily and pick up whatever fishing vehicle John had at the time, and then one of us—usually me—would drive it out to the shack so we could use it to negotiate the logging roads.

But the first time we stopped to pick up the "new" Chev, John made his remark about it being too good for me, jumped in behind the wheel, and started the engine with a roar. Almost immediately the inside of the car was full of bumblebees—hundreds of them, it seemed—and they circled John's head like fighter planes jockeying for attack position.

John, meanwhile was desperately jerking and groping for nonexistent door or window handles, and as he turned to me there was a look of horror on his face.

"JEEZUSKRISS,GETMEOUDAHERE!" John shouted.

I stood for a few seconds in amazed paralysis, and then I jerked the driver's side door open and ran like hell.

John rolled out of the Chev, stumbled to his feet, and made a "bee line" for the safety of Bill Stennis's tavern.

Bill later exterminated the bumblebees.

"I got 'em," he said the next time we went to the Wolf. "They had a nest in the back seat. I had to burn it, but you didn't need that seat anyway."

We used the old Chev some after that, but John had not only lost his original enthusiasm for it as a fishing car, he was somehow intimidated by it. So when Stennis telephoned him one day and said that a local pair of newlyweds wanted to buy the Chev so they could take a honeymoon trip to California, John agreed to sell it.

"Never did like that car," John said when I complained about his selling it. "Too damn streamlined for my taste."

I didn't ask him to explain because it wouldn't have been any use.

Bill Stennis's value as a car broker became apparent on the one occasion when John went out on the local auto market himself. He and I and my son Larry drove to the nearby town of Bryant and stopped at a garage surrounded by rusty farm implements and dented vehicles. John looked around briefly and pointed at an ancient high-wheeled pickup truck.

"Does it run?" he asked the proprietor.

When he was assured that it did, he bought it for fifty dollars, ignoring the obvious logic that in a rural community, a fifty dollar pickup has been used up.

"It will be just the thing," John said. "Look at those high wheels."

John ordered Larry to drive the pickup out to the shack, and he and I followed in my car. Larry is not a slow driver, but he drove very slowly on this trip, and when we got to the shack, he got out of the pickup rubbing at his shoulders, and with sweat running down his face.

"What's the matter?" I said.

"You can't turn the steering wheel," Larry said. "That's why I drove so slow."

"I'll show you how to drive that thing," John said, and he scrambled into the pickup and, with the engine at full roar, tried to turn it around. But he didn't have the strength for it, and after a couple of minutes he got out and said, "Take the goddamn thing in to Stennis and tell him to sell it."

Which is what we did. Bill said the next week that he could only get twenty-five dollars for it, which John said was more than it was worth.

He claimed forever afterwards that I had talked him into buying the pickup and the whole fiasco was my fault.

It was not long after that that I acquired a four-wheel drive International Scout, a vehicle that tended to have seizures whenever it crossed an angled railroad track and which rusted out so fast you could almost hear the body metal decaying.

John, however, proclaimed it the ideal vehicle for fishing the Wolf and said it was about time I took over some of the transportation responsibility.

The first time we took the Scout into the Oxbow was one of those bright Saturday mornings when the entire fishing weekend lies out there like the yellow brick road. There were four of us—John, Bob Williams, Art Jensen, and me—and we loaded all of our gear into the Scout, which had plenty of room for everything and also had a convenient split rear door so that I could latch the top open to let the set-up rods stick out over the end-gate.

We were barely into the woods when the Scout jolted over a rock in such a way that the catch on the top of the rear door tripped and the door banged down on the rod tips.

I knew immediately what had happened and I did not want to look back for confirmation.

John finally turned around to see the broken rods. "Stokes, now look what you've done," he said.

I looked, and then John was laughing and whooping and carrying on while the rest of us stared at him as if he had gone mad.

There is perhaps no connection, but once John stopped keeping a Wolf River vehicle, Claude went out of business and moved to Missouri.

I happened by one autumn day as Claude was packing up the last of his tools.

"John ruined some good old cars," Claude said, "but he never complained about a bill and he paid with cash."

Claude said he wasn't taking his old wrecker to Missouri because he had worn it out pulling John out of the woods. The last time I looked, the wrecker was sitting in the weeds out behind the old garage, a fine and appropriate monument to the days when fish cars were fish cars.

TROUT SPOOKS

ALL FISHERMEN BELIEVE in ghosts of one kind or another, and John Lawton was no exception, which explains in part why the dilapidated old farmhouse on his property near Westfield came to be known as the Haunted House. It looks the part even in the daylight, sitting in a kind of hump-backed slouch among the sighing pine at the end of a long driveway, bats squeaking in the attic, rodents burrowing in the basement, and mice scurrying through the cupboards.

That it is haunted can pretty much be attested to by anyone who has spent a night there, and that is especially true if you happen to be the sole mortal occupant. Then the ghosts are apparently challenged to wrestle your untethered imagination to a fall, and I once spent a winter night there that . . .

But that is getting ahead of the story, which begins in a way with Ed Gien. Ed, of course, was the unassuming little handyman who lived on a farm outside of Plainfield and got into trouble for robbing graves and mistaking people for deer during the Wisconsin deer season of 1957. On the opening weekend of that season, sheriff's deputies found the butchered body of one of Ed's female victims hanging in his machine shed, and they also found various items in Ed's house that had been crafted from human remains.

John, who had recently bought his sand farm some twenty miles south of Plainfield, was legal counsel for the sheriff's deputies union at the time, and some of the deputies dropped in on him at the farm as they came from viewing the horrors at the Gien place. The deputies arrived in various stages of shock and disbelief and told John about some of the incredible things they had seen, and John tried to calm them and himself with brandy. But by the time the deputies had all left, John was so nervous he said later that he went to bed without supper.

As he told it, "I started thinking about some of those bloody horrors, and I lay there rigid as a damn post."

In the middle of the night, a weather front moved through, bringing along a temperature change and gusting winds that worked on the metal roof of the house like a gang of blacksmiths.

"Damnedest noises you ever heard," John said, "and I expected some monster to come charging through the door at any minute."

In the middle of it, John's dog, a springer spaniel that was usually as unshakable as a hog, suddenly took to howling.

The next morning, friends found a bleary-eyed John hunched over the cluttered kitchen table staring at a hissing gas lantern and mumbling about things that did more than go bump in the night.

From that day forward his place was known as the Haunted House.

It is strange how fate lines things up, but the discovery of the Ed Gien horrors ultimately led to my first reporting job, and subsequently to my fishing friendship with John, which in turn brought me to the Haunted House. The Gien story became an international sensation and brought a job offer to a reporter on the *Stevens Point Daily Journal*, which was the daily closest to Plainfield. This created a vacancy that I filled when I graduated from the University of Wisconsin in the spring of 1958, with just enough journalistic sense to follow fire engines. The only Gien story that I personally covered was the burning of his house, which occurred one night to the great satisfaction of the local residents who feared that it might be turned into a tourist attraction.

My most memorable night at John's haunted house came in the dead of winter with a deep snow smothering the land. I snowshoed in one late afternoon and decided on the spur of the moment to spend the night. I was writing a newspaper column at the time and thought perhaps the night would provide some column material. It did. Before I could get to sleep in one of the side bedrooms, something opened a door on the other side of the house, and I then heard footsteps proceed in the direction of the room where—in the pitch-black of the night—I was preparing to have a heart attack.

When they got closer, I suddenly realized that the footsteps were on the ceiling! As I stared bug-eyed out into the darkness I was sure that something stared back at me, and then slowly the footsteps retreated back across the house and seemed to exit out onto the sagging old porch.

I slept that night about as much as John had on the night of Ed Gien, and later when I told John about it, he laughed and said, "Yeah, there's two or three of them. Walking around on the ceiling all the time."

There always seemed to be ghosts along the streams where John and I fished. Just below Big Slough Gundy Rapids on the Wolf there is the site of a former logging camp, and on an ancient stump on the east side of the river you can still see marks left by a broadax. The vague outline of a long-gone building can also be seen in the raised humus beneath the cedar and hemlock. And on any given night when the cedar waxwings and the brown trout are feeding on one hatch or another, if you can't hear the muted mumbling and shouting of dead lumberjacks in the roar of the rapids, then there isn't a lot to be said for the ears of your soul.

"Hell, yes, I hear them," John said once when I asked him about it. "I even hear the old whores from the Lily Hotel. They make a kind of giggling sound."

Then there was the night that John thought a big trout on the end of his line had turned into some kind of monster and was about to suck him down into the bowels of the earth. The hex hatch was on and John was back in a tamarack swamp in the middle of the night when "something" lapped up his big white fly and then dove for cover. The fish—which is what it turned out to be, of course—powered itself deep beneath an overhung bank where there was apparently an old beaver or muskrat burrow. That burrow apparently acted as a vacuum chamber when air was audibly pumped out and then sucked back in as the hooked trout fought to get away. As John described it, the result was a very eerie moaning, slurping sound, something like a malfunctioning toilet might make.

"Never heard anything like it," John said. "Scared the hell out of me because I couldn't figure out what it was."

John said he thought he might have hooked into a spirit of some kind and he entertained thoughts of dropping his rod and running like hell.

But he didn't, and the trout—a seven-pound brown which he finally landed after bulling it out from under the bank—was one of the biggest he ever caught.

There was no big trout as solace the night that John claimed that he saw either Jesus or some other high-ranking spiritualist, and it scared him so bad he wet in his waders.

It was a hot steamy night, full of mosquitoes and bats and with a dribbling hex hatch that seemed to have the trout perplexed. They fed and yet they didn't feed, and once in a while you would hear a gigantic splash made either by a beaver or a frustrated lunker trout. We were in the middle of a long swamp, thick with alder and tamarack, and between the occasional calls of barred owls and whippoorwills there were long periods of ominous silence.

"Damn strange night," John said once when I fished up behind him.

In the dim light, patches of ground fog formed to twist among the bogs, and the gurgle of the river around our waders was like the licking of sticky tongues.

I heard John fish around the bend, and then there was the silence again. Suddenly out of the gloom ahead there was a muffled curse and then something went crashing off through the swamp.

I shouted for John but there was no answer. I stood listening for a time, and then eased upstream. The river flattened out and then came together again in a sweeping curve beside a cluster of white pine trees. Then I thought I saw something move up on the far bank. A deer? Obviously a deer. But there was no alarmed snort and crashing retreat, and slowly I reached for the flashlight and snapped it on. And then I almost wet my waders.

In the yellow beam of the flashlight was the staring face of an old woman, long scraggly hair hanging down over her ears and the shadow of her nose falling across one cheek like a beak. Only her face was visible, the rest of her obscured by leaves and grass, and she didn't move an eyelash as I stared at her, the flashlight beam shining rudely in her eyes.

When my heart stopped fluttering like a wounded bird, I realized I was looking at the old woman that I had seen earlier in the farmyard near where we had parked the car. Something about her then had seemed strange, and now her specterlike appearance was downright eerie.

"Good evening," I said, finally slanting the flashlight beam away from her face.

There was no response and when I pointed the flashlight back she was gone as if she had evaporated. Then I wasn't sure she had ever been there.

I walked back to the car, stumbling in the darkness and feeling the hair on the back of my neck rise up occasionally like grouse ruff. John was there, slumped into the passenger seat with the brandy bottle in his lap.

"I saw Jesus," he said. "Scared me so bad I pissed in my waders."

"It was the old woman from the farm just up the road," I said.

"Like hell," John said. "It was Jesus or one of his people. Right there on the bank. Just the face. No body. Just a face."

"It was the old woman," I said.

John was quiet for a minute and then he said, "I suppose you're right, but by god it was an eerie damn thing to see."

We heard later that the old woman habitually roamed the countryside by day and night, frequently frightening neighbors out of their wits and becoming a witch of sorts to the community youngsters.

John and I sat there that night in the darkness sipping at the brandy and thinking about the poor old woman.

"You peed in your waders?" I said.

"Yes, damnit," John said, "but it was no big deal. I fell down earlier and they were full of water anyway."

LOVE'S LABOR LOST

NOT EVERYONE WOULD understand how I lost my fly rod one night last summer as I fought my way out of one of the Mecan River swamps. But John Lawton would have. Hell, he once lost his shotgun while hunting grouse up along the Wolf. And when it came to losing fishing gear, John was the best thing that ever happened to area tackle stores.

My fly rod debacle occurred at the end of a night of fishing that had taken me farther upstream than I had intended to go, and so the trip out through the swamp was more daunting than usual, like swimming through brush piles while blindfolded. After my rod tangled repeatedly in the vines and brush, I finally snipped off the fly and reeled in the line and leader to cut down the ensnarement potential.

That, of course, was a mistake, but by the time I realized it, the tip section of the rod was missing. I had not traveled far through the junglelike swamp, but it was far enough that I had a sinking feeling about ever finding the rod tip, particularly by the feeble beam of a faltering flashlight. To mark my location, I set the butt section of the rod—complete with reel—down next to a clump of alder and then tried to retrace my steps by noting the disturbed vegetation.

It was no use. I quickly realized that if I were ever to find the rod tip I would have to come back in the daylight. I turned around to go pick up the butt section, but it had disappeared into the clumps of dogwood and alder like a magician's wand.

I could not believe it. I had lost my entire fly rod! I floundered around a little more and then finally gave up, deciding to return in the morning.

I marked my location by whittling a ring around an alder and by breaking off several branches.

It is a humbling experience to walk back to your car after an evening of fishing and not have your fly rod along. I knew that if John had been there he would have found it a hilarious situation, but I wasn't laughing much. The rod was an expensive one that had been given to me by family members, and there was no way I could ever admit to them that I had lost it.

When I returned to the swamp in the harshness of full daylight, everything looked totally different, and there was some kind of "Rumpelstiltskin" tree fungus that made all of the trees look as if someone had carved rings around them. I spent the entire sweaty, mosquito-thick morning stumbling about in the bogs and vines, and when I was about to give up, the tip section of the rod was suddenly right there sticking up out of the nettles in front of me. With the tip in hand, I found the butt section a half hour later and crawled out of the swamp a beaten man. Whatever it was that had bedeviled John and his equipment had somehow apparently been passed on to me. I'd rather have been cursed by a coven of witches.

The circumstances of John losing his shotgun are somewhat similar to my fly rod experience. He was hunting grouse on a windy, sunny October day in the rugged hills along a section of the Wolf River. By his account, he downed a bird that crawled under a tangle of tree roots, and when he reached for it, the grouse scooted out of its hiding place and headed off through the blowing leaves. John had placed his shotgun on the ground in order to deal with the bird, and when it evaded him and he gave chase, he did not take his gun with him. The chase went on for some time.

"Every time I bent over to pick up the damn bird, it moved," John said.

When he was finally able to catch the grouse, he had no clear idea where his shotgun was.

"The wind was blowing leaves all over hell," he said, "and they had apparently covered the gun."

John went to White Lake and enlisted the help of a gaggle of high school kids, who were not sure they wanted a lot to do with a hunter who loses his gun, even though he was offering a very liberal reward for its return.

One of the young searchers finally stumbled over the gun, and John was so appreciative that he gave all of the kids a reward.

Back in the days when all fly fishermen were using bamboo, John borrowed a new three-section Orvis that his friend Hilding Haag had just bought. Just why Haag was willing to lend his new rod to John is a mystery, since everyone knew about John's propensity for equipment disaster. And predictably, when John was through fishing, he disassembled the rod so it would be easier to carry through the woods, and when he arrived back at the car, the middle section of Haag's new Orvis was gone.

Though Haag was by nature a cheerful man, his usual expression carried an air of sadness, and this was so amplified on this occasion that he looked like a whipped bloodhound.

John never went in for expensive equipment, which was a good thing since he either broke or lost a rod off the top of his car several times each season. These events did not seem to really upset him. Beyond the minor irritation of having to replace the rods, he apparently considered their loss a fact of doing business, rather like keeping tires on his car.

I don't think I ever fished with him when his waders didn't leak, and he was forever lecturing anyone who would listen about the stupidity of equipment manufacturers.

"How hard can it be to make a pair of waders that don't leak?" he would wail as he viewed the most recent rent that had resulted from the barbed wire fence he had just crawled through.

Wading sandals were also a bane to him. There was a very impressive selection of sandals under the bunks at his Wolf River cabin, but he could never find a pair that matched. "I don't understand it," he would say. "Last time they were all for the left foot and now they're all for the right."

John invariably lost one and sometimes both of his wading sandals in the river, and he spent a small fortune replacing them. Tom Alberti, who worked in the local sports shop, once asked me what John did with all the wading sandals he bought.

"He loses them," I said, and Alberti shook his head and replied, "I must have sold him a dozen pair this season."

And despite the fact that he bought more flashlights than a police department, John never had one that worked properly. "There's a conspiracy to keep me from ever having a goddamn light that works," he would moan as he twisted at a malfunctioning flashlight in the middle of a darkened trout stream.

The no-light circumstance was particularly distressing to him, of course, when there was a vigorous hex hatch going on and he couldn't see to tie on a fly. Sometimes I could hear him make a whimpering sound before exploding into a cursing shout. Sometimes then—but not all the time—I would wade to wherever he was and give him the benefit of my flashlight so he could get his gear sorted out.

For a long time, I carried in my car a "John Lawton kit," which was a blend of tools and repair material designed to make it easier to keep him functional. One time when I wired together a broken wading sandal, John said I was a mechanical wonder and could have been another Benjamin Franklin if I had only applied myself.

We were in a rural hardware store once when John picked up a metal landing net and said, "Look at the shape of that goddamn thing. How can you reach down in the rocks with a thing like that?"

And with that he grabbed the net and wrenched it into an odd oval configuration. The store proprietor had watched all of this with his mouth hanging open, and when he timidly inquired as to whether John planned to buy the net he had just remodeled, John looked at him and said, "You're damn right. It isn't every day you can find a net like that."

On another occasion John shortened a new pair of hunting pants with an ax, leaving them with one leg several inches shorter than the other and the cut edges rough and frayed. "Why the hell do they make them so long?" he said, eyeing the mangled—but shortened—pants with satisfaction.

John was equally disdainful of shirts, and whenever we were grouse hunting or fishing and he decided he had on too many clothes, he would strip off a shirt and hang it on a bush, planning to pick it up later. He never picked up a one of them, and now years later I still find an occasional rag hanging on some of the bushes where we fished or hunted.

There was one loss, however, that disturbed John for most of one summer, and which he claimed was my fault. It had to do with several hundred flies that he had worked all winter to tie. His claim that they were lost when he got them out to lend me a couple of small streamers is not true. What he lent me were nymphs.

It was our custom to get together occasionally on winter nights in John's basement to tie flies, tell lies, and sip a brandy or two, and by the opening of the trout season on this particular year, John had a choice collection of very nice flies. He was a good tier, and his flies came out of the vice with a lifelike look that I was never able to duplicate. My flies tend to look as if they have smashed themselves against a windshield. The reason for that, John once told me, was that I didn't understand enough about how a bug's brain worked, which was something he said he learned in law school. John also ridiculed me for not being able to tie a whip finish without using a device. He did it with great facility and he suggested on more than one occasion that it required a higher intelligence.

Anyway, when the trout season got underway, John had a big compartmentalized plastic container full of flies. There were at least several hundred of them in everything from tiny dries to big buggy-looking nymphs. It was early in the season, on this particular day, and we had been fishing the Wedde. I had been shut out, but John had caught a couple of small browns on nymphs and so once back at the parking lot

I asked him about his nymph selection. He pawed around in his flies for a minute or two and finally handed me a couple of medium-sized nymphs, with the admonition that those were the last ones I was going to get.

We drove off toward the Mecan and when we arrived at the bridge, John could not find his big fly box.

"I'm sure I put it back in the car after I gave you those flies," he said, throwing gear around in a searching frenzy.

He hadn't, of course, and when we got back into the car and retraced our route, we found the fly box in the ditch. There was not a fly in it. Not one.

John had left the box on top of the car, and the flies had all scattered to the wind before the box itself finally blew off.

John slumped down in the car seat and said, "All winter. I worked on those flies all winter."

I didn't say anything.

"It's your fault, Stokes," John said. "If you hadn't been begging for flies like a goddamn puppy it wouldn't have happened."

We sat there beside the road for a while, and then John started laughing and whooping loud enough to alarm the sandhill cranes.

"Serves me right, for the company I keep," he said, and then he laughed again until tears ran down his cheeks.

At least I think he was laughing.

WESTERN GAS

WHILE A CERTAIN earthiness must be tolerated if accounts of fishing excursions are to have the ring of authenticity, some experiences pose special challenges in this regard. The one and only western fishing trip that John Lawton and I made together is a case in point.

At the center of this is society's inability to deal matter-of-factly with the eternal verity that the human body in its normal functioning produces a certain amount of gas. The final, inevitable result of this very natural and very necessary activity not only has no cultural respect whatsoever, it has been elevated to such comic status that it has its own icon—the whoopee cushion. And John Lawton seemed to take special delight in jumping up and down on society's whoopee cushion at the slightest provocation. Frequently this took the form of impromptu lectures.

"History tells us," he would say, "that people did not always live in a society of absurd denial but in some previous ages a certain expression of comfort and approval could be inferred in the audible relief from a gas buildup."

Sometimes it was hard to stop him when he got going on this theme, and he would expound like a verbose schoolboy, stopping only to laugh and replenish his brandy glass. It is this attitude that probably made the debacle in the rancher's yard that September afternoon worse than it otherwise might have been.

John, my adult son Larry, and I had been fishing in and around Yellowstone with mixed success when John suddenly announced that he remembered a river he had fished as a kid growing up in Montana. We should go there immediately, John said, adding that the river was full of big trout.

It was a long drive from where we were, but the next morning we started out, stopping once to fish briefly and unsuccessfully where a stream snaked up against the road, and arriving in the general area of John's remembered river about noon. We stopped for lunch at a roadside picnic table, and Larry broke out the camp stove and heated up a big can of beans and chili that we had bought earlier. I remember glancing at the can and thinking that it was an unfamiliar brand, but it tasted all right, and John and I wolfed down generous portions while drinking warm beer. Larry, in the meantime, decided that he did not like the beans and chili and ate something else.

We loaded up again, and as we drove along the roads that John said would take us to our destination, a strange rumbling sensation developed in my stomach.

"You feel okay?" I asked the others.

"Feel fine," Larry said.

"My gut's funny," John said.

"Mine too," I said. "It must have been those chili beans."

We made several wrong turns, or at least John said they were wrong, and as we bumped up and down over the dusty back roads, a full-scale storm developed in my gut. Apparently in John's too, because he rubbed his stomach and cursed as he peered out through the dirty windshield.

Suddenly, though, he sat up straight and said, "This is it. I remember the gate."

I didn't tell him that the gate at the ranch driveway he had indicated was made of fairly new lumber and couldn't possibly have been around when he was a kid. Who knows, maybe the rancher had replicated the old gate.

As we got out of the car, our respective systems suddenly began such an unexpected and sustained expulsion of gas that we were both more or less speechless. We looked at each other, and in his anticipation of resurrecting a childhood fishing experience, John ignored the potential for schoolboy humor and said, "Come on. Let's go talk to the rancher."

Larry, perhaps with some sense of impending disaster, said he would stay with the car, and John and I started down the driveway. As we did so, the condition of our digestive systems deteriorated to the point that we sounded like a parade of trombones.

"My god," John said. "Never had anything like it."

Nor had I. A chemical reaction of awesome proportions had obviously seized our insides and we were absolutely helpless before it. Even at the rate it was being expelled, there seemed to be reason for concern that the gas might build up to explosive proportions, and a vague image of what this might portend flashed through my mind.

At the ranch house porch we tried to resume control of things, but we succeeded only long enough for John to rap his knuckles on the wall. A woman opened the door, and as John smiled at her and asked for her husband, he also broke wind loud enough to startle the chickens. The woman stared at him, pointed toward a shed, and then quickly shut the door.

"I couldn't help it," John said, and I understood because as we walked toward the shed both of us became trombones again. We exchanged looks, and John only half succeeded in keeping a sober face on matters.

"Those must have been poison beans," he said, and I agreed. "We should probably see a doctor," John said, but he kept walking.

Just how he planned to carry on a conversation with the rancher was beyond me, and he was apparently thinking along the same lines because he said, "We just can't get too close."

As we stepped around the corner of the shed, we saw the rancher tinkering with a hay baler. He looked up, and though we were thirty feet from him, we both stopped and shouted a greeting.

"Howdy," the rancher said, and motioned for us to approach.

There was no way either of us could quell the thunderous turmoil in our guts and we stayed where we were as John tried to introduce himself and inquire about fishing opportunity.

The rancher stared at us with a puzzled expression, wondering obviously why we didn't come over and shake hands and talk to him face to face. As our uncontrollable gas problem continued to produce a trombonelike duet, John shouted, "We're looking for a place to fish," and as he spoke he began to giggle, softly at first and then louder.

This really seemed to get the rancher's attention and he stood up straight and craned his neck toward us. John's laughter built gradually until it was as out of control as his gas problem. And then both of us were laughing and . . . well, sounding like a couple of overfed horses, while the rancher backed up a couple of steps and glanced toward his house.

John was beyond any attempts at conversation, and between fits of choking laughter and very loud expulsions of gas, he waved a hand at the rancher and gave a kind of helpless shrug as we turned and began a retreat back toward the car.

We passed the ranch house and saw the rancher's wife duck back away from a kitchen window, and then we were in full and helpless retreat. Larry heard us coming, and opened the car doors so that we fell into the vehicle like besotted drunks, still hooting with laughter and still making those other sounds.

"Get us out of here before he calls the sheriff," John gasped between waves of laughter and flatulence.

It was at least an hour before our gas attacks subsided, and between them and our laughing we were too weak to even think about fishing.

"What the hell caused something like that?" John said later.

"Don't know," I said, "but I've never experienced anything like it."

"Me neither," John said, "and I feel bad about the way we treated that rancher."

"We could go back and try to explain and apologize," I said.

But of course we didn't. Some things simply defy explanation.

There were other things to remember about our western trip. John said at one campsite we didn't have to worry about grizzly bears because this wasn't their territory. The next day at a ranger station a half mile down the road they displayed a plaster cast of a bear track as big as a manhole cover.

In a Jackson Hole sports shop, John bought a pair of metal-spiked wading sandals that caught on shoreline rocks the first time he put them on and he did a kind of off-balance dance that produced sparks and odd clatter.

I got lost one night returning from the river and as it got later and later, Larry became convinced that some dire fate had befallen me. "Oh, he's all right," John told Larry. "Have a drink, and if he isn't here by the time it's gone, it will be safe to drink his share of the brandy."

Larry said later that he stopped worrying immediately.

We got stuck in a high altitude snowstorm, and there were a number of other memorable occurrences. But the thing that identifies that trip was our sudden gas attack and the way it interfered with what could have been some fantastic fishing.

That doesn't seem like the way you should remember a trout fishing trip to the glorious mountains, and it is probably just as well that we went only that one time.

OFF SEASON

IT IS PROBABLY a good thing that the cycle of seasons in Wisconsin dictates only four or five months of trout fishing, and that is especially true if you fished with someone like John Lawton. By the time red and yellow leaves were tumbling through the trout pools like the coinage of a spendthrift summer, John was in something of a collapse and decay of his own. This, of course, carried over to those who spent time with him. When the trout season finally wound down, John's waders were in shreds, his fly rod was taped together, most of his flies had long since been lost, and his fly vest looked like a very old road kill. I'm sure that I was not as decrepit as he was, but certainly by September I was not what you would call fresh off the angling bench, and toward the end of the hopper season, it was sometimes a downright chore to keep things together enough to enjoy fishing.

It was therefore almost a relief to put down the trout gear and pick up the paraphernalia of grouse hunting. Such feelings, producing as they do an unfailing blush of initial enthusiasm, must relate to something deep in our bones. Perhaps the allure of seasonal change touches the residual fragments of the urge to migrate, a trait that—each fall when the geese cry overhead—we seem to regret having handed off to the birds.

One bright, cool autumn afternoon, John and I stood in the clutter of the yard at the Haunted House and watched hundreds of sandhill cranes assemble in small, trumpeting flocks as they rode thermals until the birds were mere specks in the sky. Then the cranes would suddenly peel out of their aerial elevator and sail off like arrows toward the next thermal far to the south.

It was like watching the summer and the trout season disappear into a series of spectral whirlpools, and we stood and watched it in awed silence.

While most grouse hunters would claim that their sport is enhanced by the company of dogs—and John and I would probably have agreed with that—the brutal truth is that our hunting was more or less encumbered by dogs. We each had a male springer spaniel and these dogs hated each other like rival gunfighters. This meant that if we were to hunt together, one or the other of us would have to start off with his dog and get almost out of sight before the other could turn his dog loose and head out to join the hunt. Once the hunt was underway, the dogs pretty much behaved themselves, carefully avoiding each other as they plowed through the swamps and creek bottoms. Sometimes there would be a growling harangue if John or I shot a grouse and both dogs responded to the sound of the shotgun. But these disputes were pretty much just "verbal." John and I could never get together to talk things over during a hunt because it would lead inevitably to a dog fight. As a result, we would stand on opposite hillsides or across the creek from each other and shout back and forth in order to plan our next move.

It was, of course, necessary for us to drive separate vehicles because putting both of those cantankerous springers into the same car would have been like tossing two tom cats into a barrel. One very rainy, soggy day at the parking lot along Lawrence Creek, John had his dog shut in the car while I and my dog got ready to begin our hunt. John's dog, as usual, was incensed by this turn of events and it began to bark and snarl viciously and run in tight circles around the inside of the car. In his imprisoned frenzy the dog's paws pushed down all of the car's door locks. The car keys were, of course, inside in the ignition. I was not aware of any of this unfortunate circumstance as I headed off into the sodden woods.

It was not until much later—after I had taken a bird out of the first grouse covey—that I realized John had not shown up to hunt. I circled back to the car to find John trying to pry open a window so he could get at his shotgun. He said he planned to shoot his dog, but he didn't mean it. Instead he cursed and laughed and said that since I was the mechanical one, why didn't I show him how to get into his car.

It was finally necessary to break one of the vent windows, and it did not occur to me until it was too late that it would have been better to have broken the one on the passenger side. John realized this before I did, and said I was dumber than his dog, and now how the hell was he supposed to keep from being drenched by the rain?

Most of the time we hunted the creek bottoms and adjoining swamps, and occasionally in October we would happen onto a shallow gravel bar where the brook trout would be spawning, sometimes good-sized regal fish that were like exquisite jewelry in the clear sparkling water. Then we would stand and watch them, until the dog fight started, which we always broke up by heading away from the dogs in opposite directions. As much as they liked to fight, the springers were apparently more concerned with being left out of the hunt.

On one of our grouse hunts, we were joined by a young doctor who had just gotten his pointer back from an expensive training facility in Canada. There was a certain amount of challenging dog juggling necessary to get the three-dog hunt underway, but finally the good doctor fastened a little silver bell onto his dog's collar and let him go. There was a sudden ding-ding-ding that quickly faded from hearing—like a Good Humor man going off into the next neighborhood—and that is the last we saw of the pointer all day.

"That dog was trained to hunt in Canada, and by god, that's where he's gone," John told the chagrined doctor.

Our springers, meanwhile, had been into three or four brief but noisy fights, and that may have been what influenced the pointer to head for Canada.

Our doctor pal found his dog two days later at a farm where it had been befriended by a female collie. Neither the doctor nor his dog ever expressed any desire to hunt with us again.

The grouse hunt was always interrupted by the deer season, and John's attitude toward deer hunting was pretty much wrapped up in his labeling of those who hung around his Haunted House during the deer season as "a pack of assholes."

Nobody took offense at this. In fact the appellation was accepted with a certain amount of pride. Given the huge deer herd in Wisconsin—well over a million animals—and the three-quarters of a million people who chase after them each year, the season is more of a shoot than a hunt. As a result, those who participate must be restrained from taking themselves too seriously. John certainly did his part in that regard, holding forth at the old round table in his kitchen like a saloon judge, ridiculing the fumbling attempts at "harvesting" the bumper crop of deer that roamed his acreage and daring anyone to claim any special prowess from having killed a deer.

"Easier than shooting one of Art Sharnberg's cows," John would say, Sharnberg being the farmer out at the end of John's driveway.

John's role during the deer shoot—when he wasn't presiding over his kitchen court—was to take a shotgun and his springer spaniel and roam up and down the creek bottom looking for grouse.

"I'll make a drive for you assholes," he would announce. "Get on your stands."

This almost always produced deer, and one year on the last afternoon of the season I shot the biggest buck of my life when it came thundering out of the creek bottom ahead of John and his dog. It was, for me, a spectacular shot that dropped the leaping animal from a considerable distance. But when I tried to point this out to John, he hooted and said the deer ran so close to me that I killed it in self-defense. He also suggested that the deer might have been half tame because it had been hanging around the creek all summer where he fished.

"That buck snorted at me every time I was down by the creek," John said. "Poor old thing probably figured you were just another harmless trout fisherman."

In what turned out to be an embarrassing incident, John and I once invited a friend of mine named Harvey up for opening weekend of the deer season and then forgot that we were supposed to meet him down at the corner and show him the way to the Haunted House. Two days later we happened onto Harvey during a deer drive. He was meandering about rather aimlessly in the woods, and his manner was somewhat restrained. John didn't help matters by pointing out that I didn't deserve to have any friends if that was the way I was going to treat them.

"You forgot him?" John said with mock incredulity, and then he went into a fit of roaring laughter.

I still have guilt pangs about Harvey.

John's limited tolerance for deer shooters did not carry over to snowmobilers. John seemed to consider the advent of the snowmobile to be an insult to winter, a noisy, smelly device that demeaned a season noted for its silent challenges and cold, pure character. John was an early cross-country skier, and I once saw him nearly create a shishkebab with one of his ski poles and a snowmobiler who had the poor judgment to come roaring down one of John's trails in a cloud of flying snow.

"Worst goddamn thing ever invented," John grumbled later.

The snowmobile came on the scene about the time that John and I got into something of a contest about who could sleep outside on the snow under the coldest conditions. He claimed he had outclassed me on a night when the temperature dropped to twenty below and he slept out under the jackpine with his dog, both of them in the same sleeping bag. Then one day in late January I found myself in the northern part of the state and rode the snowshoes in over four feet of snow to spend the night in a deer yard when the thermometer read thirty below. I had no idea it was going to get that cold, and though the night was an exciting experience, I had doubts about my sanity the next morning when my hands suddenly got so cold I could not buckle on the snowshoes.

I wrote a newspaper feature story about that night, but John said he didn't believe any of it and that I had made it all up from the comfort of a motel room.

So the off-season went, and then slowly the brutal temperatures would ease off, and finally the snow would melt, and the trout fishing fever would be upon us again.

There would be boxes of freshly tied flies, and John would haunt the sports shop and buy all kinds of new equipment, some of which he would somehow lose even before the trout season started, and there would be telephone calls about where and how we should open the season.

Usually the decision was to go to the Wolf, though winter always seemed to linger longest in that rugged part of the state. One year when we arrived to find that a family of snowshoe rabbits had made their winter home under the Wolf River shack, a bitter wind froze us off the river, and we retreated to the shack. As we hovered around the rusty old stove, a sudden snow squall blew in and I looked out the window to see several rabbits hopping through the flying snowflakes in the general direction of the shack.

When I called his attention to the advancing rabbits, John cursed the weather and said, "Open the door, the poor bastards want to come in and get warm."

It was a typical trout opener, but anything is better than the off-season.

SHOULD AULD. . .

WHEN CHAPMAN billies leave the street,
And drouthy neibors neibors meet,
As market days are wearin' late,
And folk begin to tak the gate,
While we sit bousing at the nappy,
And gettin' fou and unco happy,
We think na on the long Scots miles,
The mosses, waters, slaps and stiles . . .

Thus would begin John Lawton's campfire rendition of "Tam o' Shanter," the Robert Burns poem about the infamous character who let his pleasures get the upper hand. John's poetry performance always seemed like a fitting way to top off a day of trout fishing that had invariably been marked by some great plan gone awry, or a series of senseless disasters.

John would stand with a brandy glass in hand, the light of the fire bouncing off his face, and recite verse after verse, and to the backdrop of calling whippoorwills and barred owls, his enthusiastic recitation would transport his listeners to that wild, haunted Scottish night as certainly as the witches flew out of Kirk-Alloway.

Sometimes he would get through the entire poem, and these occasions seemed to give him great satisfaction. Other times he would be swept up in the hilarity of Tam's dilemma and double over in a laughing fit that would make him forget the rest of the poem.

Anyone who immersed himself so deeply in the frivolity of trout fishing, as John did, obviously saw a kindred soul in poor old Tam.

And if John had a theme song it was Burns's "My Heart's in the Highlands," which he would order me to sing at odd times, such as when we would first arrive at his Wolf River shack for a weekend of fishing. While I can carry a tune, I am no Pavarotti, but when I belted out that old song with enough enthusiasm to quiet the wood thrushes, John would say, "By god, Stokes, that was beautiful."

It is rather a shame that John and Robert Burns could not have been traveling companions through life's travail. The material that John could have provided the poet would have inspired him to even greater heights. I can imagine, for example, a poem entitled, "Upon Lying Down with Woodticks."

We were fishing the Wolf early in the season and a sudden heat wave descended over the river bottom as we worked wet flies among the boulders. The strength of the current in the deep slicks made it hard work, and there wasn't enough fish action to take our minds off this fact, so we hauled ourselves out of the river to rest. Beside the logging road that followed the river, there was the collapsed remains of a log stable where a pulp cutter from winters past had kept his horse. Next to this pile of debris was a heap of decaying straw that obviously appealed to John as an opportune mattress for a midday snooze. He flung himself down on it and was snoring within seconds.

I always envied John his ability to seemingly command sleep whenever the opportunity arose. I swear he could grab a nap while waiting for a traffic light. On this occasion, however, his talent for descending to oblivion would have to be considered a liability. Unbeknownst to John, the straw mattress he lay down on had earlier been appropriated by hundreds of woodticks that, being opportunists in their own right, began an immediate advance onto and into John's warm body.

I was sitting with my back against a cedar tree, when I noticed that John began to squirm, slowly at first, and then more vigorously until he was virtually writhing around on top of the straw heap.

It was a curious thing to see, and as I watched, he suddenly sat bolt upright, his eyes bugged out and his mouth slightly open.

"JEEZUS KEERIST!" he shouted, and leaped to his feet and began to strip off his waders and rip at his clothes.

His body was covered with woodticks. He danced around in a half-naked state, plucking at himself and cursing, and if I hadn't been rolling around in laughter I would have helped him with his tick harvest.

What would Burns have made of that?

Oh wad some power the giftie gie us
To see oursels as ithers see us!
Covered o'r with creep and sprawl
Wile ithers laugh with boundless gall!

Certainly the great poet could have done better. And he could also have written wondrously about John dancing in his waders at the School House tavern. This happened one day when we were driving from one stream to another and stopped at the tavern so John could run in for a six-pack of cold beer. I waited in the car and when he didn't show up after fifteen minutes I went in to check on him.

It took a while for my eyes to adjust to the dim tavern lighting, but finally I saw a large woman in a flowered dress swinging John around by his wader suspenders as both of them whooped with laughter.

John explained later that he knew the woman from having done some legal work for her years back and that she had grabbed him as he came in the door and wouldn't let go.

"Damn good thing you came in," John said later. "I couldn't have gotten away from her on my own."

John delighted in relating these kinds of outrageous experiences to his wife, Esther, when he returned home, and she would join him in the kind of laughter that cements good marriages. Esther was stricken with multiple sclerosis not long after John and I started fishing together, and for many years she was restricted to the house and finally to her bed. Through the years John maintained constant telephone contact with her, sometimes going to great effort to get to a telephone to see how Esther was doing and to report our misfortunes.

Once when I visited them at their home on the tail end of a Thanksgiving weekend, John's springer spaniel suddenly appeared in the living room door with the entire turkey carcass in his mouth. The dog stood there staring out over the turkey skeleton, and in the uproar of laughter that followed I never did learn whether the dog had fished the turkey out of the garbage or filched it off the table.

But Esther and John's mirthful reaction to the incident was typical of the spirit that prevailed in their home despite the debilitating handicap that controlled them both.

As Esther's condition worsened with the years, John's kidneys began to fail him, and he began a long regimen of treatment that ultimately saw him using a portable dialysis machine. Given his incompetence with all things mechanical, this was akin to putting a cat on a motor scooter. But he persevered, and while his condition slowly deteriorated, he hung in there, even to the extent of fly fishing that last summer. That maintaining his status was in part an act of will in order to look after Esther is beyond doubt. But then Esther died and things began to change.

One Saturday morning there was a ceremony at an intersection along the Tagatz Creek at which a section of the creek was dedicated as the John A. Lawton Fishery. All kinds of state dignitaries were there, including most of the Department of Natural Resources board members that John had served with, and former governor Tony Earl who had appointed him.

John was weak but able to stand up and grin as the few brief speeches were made. He stood by the new wooden designation sign with his daughter and son and grandchildren as people snapped photos, and then everyone retired to the Westfield fish hatchery for refreshments. I didn't stay long because, damnit, it was a warm day and an afternoon caddis hatch was practically guaranteed. John would have expected me to fish it.

From that point on it was all downstream for John. He was in and out of the hospital, and the last time I went to see him, he was barely able to laugh. But he managed it, at least a few chuckles as I recalled some of the times we had shared together.

A night or so later his daughter Jeannie called and said he was gone.

Robert Burns's most recognizable song was appropriate for that evening, as it is now as I close out this rambling account of the best goddamn fishing pal a man ever had:

Should auld acquaintance be forgot,
And never brought to min'?
Should auld acquaintance be forgot,
And days o' auld lang syne.

For auld lang syne, my dear,
For auld lang syne,
We'll tak a cup o' kindness yet
For auld lang syne.

NEW OLD GUY

"WHAT GOES AROUND . . . " and all of that.

So now I am no longer the kid or the junior companion but "the old guy" of the trout outings. I do not understand how that happened. It was only yesterday that I was following one of those grizzled old goats along the sun-washed rivers of my youth, or stumbling along behind long-time fishing friend John Lawton as we navigated a Wolf River rapids.

Now? Now it is grinning grandchildren who follow me. Some of them treading in the footsteps of their fathers, but for some of the others whose fathers are not so much into fishing, it is in my company that these innocents are getting their initial exposure to trout joys and frustrations.

While all of my kids—four sons and a daughter—enjoy fishing, only one son, Larry, has so far been rendered totally foolish by the trout fishing bug. That bug bit him one sunny Sunday afternoon when he was about fifteen and he and I waded up the Mecan River and I pointed out a feeding brown that he promptly caught on a badly thrown Adams.

The trout hook apparently went as deep into Larry as it did into the brown that day, and once he managed to navigate the treacherous waters of the "spawning" years, Larry came back to trout fishing like a hungry bear. My other offspring were exposed to similar experiences, but they have been able to keep trout fishing in perspective, which, I tell them, makes me doubt their lineage.

While I do not understand how time flew by so fast, I accept the fact that "nae man can tether time nor tide," and dwelling on my change in fishing status would be as silly as being morose about the gray in my mustache. And, truth be known, this angling seniority has its perks, not the least of which is a general disinclination to be held totally accountable.

I took a couple of grandsons, Nick and Tony, on a trout fishing excursion a couple of summers ago in which I tried to find the beaver pond where Wayne Yureko had taken me as a boy. Wayne and I had caught so many beautiful brook trout from that pond that there had to be some of them left. There weren't, of course. There wasn't even a pond, and in the course of our struggle through some of the worst muck and mire imaginable, the boys and I found ourselves apparently stranded on a point of land from which the only retreat was to crawl on hands and knees through a quarter mile of blackberry briars that had sprouted up after a recent pulpwood cut.

In retrospect, accepting that formidable blackberry challenge might have been the wiser choice because when we tried to follow the stream to get back to the road, we got stuck in the kind of water-covered loon shit that seemed to go on through the stumps and snags forever.

Nick and Tony were heroic in their efforts to stay with me, and they did so pretty much without complaint, though at one point as he floundered through the mire amid clouds of savage mosquitoes, Tony said, "Hey, Pa-B, think we'll get out of here before it gets dark?"

We did, of course. What kind of grandfather would get trapped with his grandchildren after dark in the primordial soup of a trout swamp! We were out of there with at least twenty minutes of daylight to spare.

Two other grandsons, Andy and Steve, joined me a couple of years ago on a trip to the Ignace, Ontario, area, and we spent a wonderful week doing all of the weird things that go along with such an outing. We arrived in the midst of a late spring snowstorm, got wet and stuck, shivered in wind-tossed boats, and caught enough northern pike to make some delicious shore lunches. We also explored some of the towering ridges of bedrock, and on top of one of them we were able to knock the stops out from under a huge boulder so that it went crashing and thundering down the slope like an echoing remnant of the glacier that had originally left it on its precarious perch. The boulder plunged finally into the lake with a mighty splash that had us all cheering.

"Awesome," Andy said.

One day we followed a stream to a hidden lake and stood on the boggy shores knowing that if we could only get out there to fish it we would catch tons of huge lake trout. Next time, we vowed, we would bring in a canoe.

We saw a moose and her calf and several beaver, and we sat around the campfire in the evenings and the boys had to listen to the adults tell stories that everyone else had heard a dozen times.

The week went by like a minute, and Andy and Steve wanted to know on the way home if we could do it again next year.

It isn't all grandsons that now fill the fishing ranks. At our cabin one weekend recently, thirteen-year-old granddaughter Jessie caught a sixteen-inch brook trout that I had been after all season.

"It was pretty easy, actually," Jessie said.

I told her she was no longer permitted to fish with worms, but Jessie just gave me that Mona Lisa smile of hers as she posed for a photograph with her dad and the trout.

I have never caught a brook trout that big out of our stream, but I didn't tell that to Jessie.

Last summer I hooked a small travel trailer behind my Ford van and loaded up four of my grandsons—Nick, Tony, Andy, and Steve—for a few days with the trout rivers of northeast Wisconsin. We went first to the Wolf, of course, my vehicle more or less heading there from habit. The boys wiggled into waders and we all fished up through Big and Little Slough Gundy Rapids, catching only a couple of little browns and a small bass or two.

We stopped briefly at John Lawton's shack where he and I had spent so many wonderful hours, and the boys read the penciled notes we had made over the years on the cedar walls.

"Didn't you guys ever catch anything?" Nick asked at one point as he noted the repeated notations about high water or no hatches or days of stormy weather.

We camped one night at the Wolf, and left the next morning to set up in a Forest Service park that gave us general access to such rivers as the Pine and Popple and Peshtigo. We hit them all, but our timing was bad since the doldrums of summer had slowed fishing until we were forced to eat hamburger. But we waded up and down some magnificient rivers, and we saw some great country and had some great campfires. And given the circumstances, the temptation was too great for me to resist telling the boys about such things as my army experiences and various other fascinating aspects of my life.

I thought I was being careful not to go on so long that I bored them, but then I saw Steve dozing off as he sat on a log across the campfire, and I gave up on the combat stories.

"Tell us about the time you and my dad and Uncle Scott canoed down the Wisconsin River," Tony said.

"Yeah and how the storm blew away your tent and all your supplies," Steve said.

"How about that time you were with Uncle Mike and Rick, and you got your ankles sunburned and couldn't walk and Nana had to come and get you?" Andy said.

"Dad told us that once when he and Aunt Pat were real little you took them fishing and you fell in over your head because you said it wasn't deep there," Nick said. "Is that true?"

"Tell us about that," Tony said.

So I told them all of those stories that they were primed to laugh at, and the sound of that laughter as it floated out into the summer darkness was like some incomparable balm that made me sleep that night like a puppy.

As we worked river after river, the only fly that seemed to produce even little trout for me was a small silver-sided streamer, and once I told the boys this, they agreed to do absolutely all of the work the rest of the trip if I would tie them some of those streamers. According to the terms of the deal that was struck, I should not have had to do so much as fill my own coffee cup for the duration of our outing. I was able to hold them to the terms of our contract until they had proven to themselves that the silver streamers didn't catch fish for them either, and then they said that I could get my own coffee.

We stopped at the casino in Keshena on the way back to the Wolf River, and the boys insisted that I take along five dollars of their money and invest it on the blackjack table. Later when I reported back to them in the van where they waited, they seemed to be philosophical about that fact that I had lost my money and theirs.

"We were planning to buy you something really nice with our winnings," Nick said.

"Yeah," Andy said, "like a new fly rod."

Back at the Wolf, Nick caught a nice hefty brown and I managed to coax another one into taking a big crawfish imitation. So I was able to cook up that one trout supper, which the boys said was better than hamburger, but they might have been humoring the chef.

On a more recent trip to the Wolf, Larry, Nick, Tony, and I spent a week fishing out of John's shack and had a couple of evenings on the Oxbow when the brown drake hatch provided the kind of action that trout fishers dream about. I sat on the bank at one point and watched Tony struggle with a huge brown which he ultimately brought to the net.

"Look, Pa-B," Tony shouted as he hefted the fish.

"Beautiful!" I shouted back, and watched as Tony released the trout.

And in that moment, with the river shadows taking on that special twilight depth, I remembered that it was not far from here that much of the trout fishing nonsense began. It did not take a lot of imagination to hear John Lawton's laughter in the gurgle of the river, or to see his floundering form across the current in the maze of big boulders.

Like all fishing trips, this one was obviously not measured in terms of the fish it produced. There were all those other things.

This is, of course, the technique that outdoor writers depend on to fill space, and during my tenure on that beat, I honed that skill to an art. So perhaps that is what is going on here, and maybe it is what has gone on during all of the time that I was metamorphosing as a fisherman from a pink-cheeked innocent into a tribal elder. The focus was not on fish, certainly, because most often there were not enough of them to focus on. Instead, in the grand outdoor writer tradition of filling in with sunsets and serenity and socializing, attention has been diverted and direction skewed.

I make no apology for that. We all understand that fishing is not really about catching fish, and that the joys involved in learning this verity from our predecessors and passing it on to the kids is the real magic of it all.

So we'll end it here, on a June evening on the banks of the Wolf, with a grandson catching a big trout and me sneaking a sip of brandy and feeling like God.